FOREV

A friend of mine who has worked in the oil industry tells u.. of a
saying there that runs like this: 'The first generation of an oil company
is made up of oil finders, the second generation is made up of managers,
the third generation is made up of accountants and the fourth-generation,
lawyers. There is no fifth generation.' It's a saying that could be easily
transferred to churches and even denominations. It's all too easy for us
as individuals and organisations to slip into a state of spiritual flabbiness
where, although we seem to be believing the same things we always did,
we're not actually living them out in the way we once did. It's a common
but ultimately fatal disease. In the last few decades the evangelical faith
has made enormous progress in Britain and elsewhere. We now have a
formidable scholarship, tremendous conferences, stunning musicians and
brilliant websites. We are involved in social issues and are – quite
commonly – treated seriously by politicians and the media. It's really
encouraging. And yet sometimes I look around and I wonder, 'Where's
the fire?' It seems to me that in the same way that it is possible for oil
companies to lose that most fundamental ability of finding oil, so it is
possible for evangelical Christians to lose the ability to share the gospel.
And in the same way, an evangelical faith that is no longer evangelistic
will very soon cease to be evangelical.

It's on that basis I welcome this book. It seems to me full of what
you might call Vitamin E, a substance that is utterly essential for a vigorous
life.

There is **Energy** here. We all know the sad definition of those later
stages of life where the 'get up and go has got up and gone'. Sadly, there
are many Christians for whom the phrase can be used in a spiritual sense.
Well there is a lot of energy here, and it's a great reminder that if we
believe the good news of Christ and know something of the presence
and power of his Spirit, then we need to be those who are active and
lively in sharing the gospel.

I

myself.' I'd been trying to do everything in my own strength, but sometimes we just need to say, 'Help. Father, forgive me for trying to fix myself. Please help me.' As soon as I prayed that prayer, the power of God came on me. The anointing. The gift of faith. Hallelujah. Don't deny the power.

Once I'd prayed that prayer the rest of the holiday was great. It says in 2 Corinthians 3:18 that God takes us from glory to glory. But sometimes as we go from glory to glory, in between each level there's generally a level of gory – times of challenge or pain.

We came back from that holiday and within a day I'd got a voicemail from a lady asking me to call her back. I started weeping. I had a good idea what it was. I rang back. The lady said, 'We've got it. We've got half a million pounds worth of funding.' Glory to God. Don't deny the gift of faith. We do what we can do but we must allow God to do what only he can do.

Shortly after that I stood outside a building in Surrey. It contained twenty-four two-bedroom flats that must have been worth a quarter of a million each. As I stood outside I started weeping under the anointing. I knew the gift of faith had come upon me. I said to Jill, 'We're going to get those flats.' Miraculously, within months, they were ours. We got all the equipment in and twenty-four young homeless people in there. Glory to God.

Things just grew. Within a short space of time we got another ten or eleven buildings and 250 members of staff transferred into our organisation. Huge, massive growth. Huge.

Not long after that the Lord moved us on and we came back up North. It can be a bit gory when you're moving on from one season to the next, if we're all honest. If we're not connected to the Lord and trusting in what the Lord's given us, it becomes quite a dangerous place, guys, I'll tell you. Everything can be taken away, apart from our relationship with Jesus, apart from the anointing.

No matter how successful you become in the rat race, you're still a rat. Do you understand that quote? Even on the 'who's who' of the charismatic zoo wheel, you can just become another rat in the rat race, just running around, jumping from one thing to the next thing to another.

You get burned out with it all. It's so important to stay under the anointing. Stay under the gift of faith and get our security in God. Let him give us what he wants to give us. Hold things lightly.

GOD'S PLAN FOR MY LIFE

A couple of years ago we were up North and I was thinking about what I should be doing. Should I keep going with property? I was also involved in the music business, should I keep going with that? What about evangelism and ministry? Shall we do all these things? The Lord clearly spoke to me in Bulgaria about just going with the gift of evangelism. Shortly after that doors opened up again. I've got the gift of faith. Doors opened up with some cool ministry teams – Compassion UK, UCB, amongst others. Don't deny the power, guys. God loves us. Jesus died for us. He's got a plan for our lives. And what God's got for you, no one can take away from you. No man, no devil in hell. God loves you. Jesus died for you. He's got a plan for your life.

Recently I was invited to visit Whitemoor Prison, a Category A maximum security prison. It's a prison for people doing ten, fifteen years and over. It's a dangerous place. The chaplain contacted me and said, 'I've seen your material. The Lord's told me to invite you in.' I said, 'Great.' He said, 'We've been seeing all these guys saved here. We've got about fifty men on fire for God.' I thought *Wow!*

It came time for me to go in there and it was all very intimidating and imposing. When I got to the chapel there was a revival service going on! I'll tell you, the people there were worshipping God, worshipping Jesus like they knew him personally. They loved him with all their heart. Absolutely powerful. The worship music stopped because the computer broke down and all you heard was this chorus of men just worshipping Jesus. It was so powerful. The chaplain got up and started by asking if anybody would like to testify. They were all coming up to testify. These guys were getting saved, filled with the power of God, speaking in tongues, doing the work of the evangelist in the prison. When I'd finished speaking to them I said, 'I could go on all day. I could tell you stories like this all day.' They replied with, 'Come on, Terry, preach it.' They were so keen to hear the Word of God. I went, 'OK, one more . . .' and I was preaching again.

We did an altar call and the altar was absolutely full of people. The prison officers at the back had their heads bowed. God was touching these guys. By the time we left there were seventy men all on fire for God, hungry for God. I'm telling you, if you shook these guys out across the United Kingdom we'd see a revival in this nation. The Lord told me about fifteen years ago that we're on the verge of the greatest revival this nation has ever seen. He said, 'I'm going to take people whose lives have been completely written off and I'm going to write them back on and use them for my glory, and they'll be the greatest evangelists this nation has ever seen.' I didn't see anything happening for a while but then four years ago I started meeting people around the UK: ex-drug addicts, ex-gangsters, ex-this, ex-that. God is doing a work in this nation, guys, and we are a big part of it.

On the back of my visit to Whitemoor, I was invited to the National Prison Fellowship Conference in Derbyshire. I spoke to people from all around the nation, saw them ignited by the power of God. We had over half of the people at the altar at the end. Amazing. We saw high-ranking government officials saved. Following on from that I was asked to speak at the Regional Prison Fellowship in London and the Regional Fellowship in Cornwall.

A little while ago I started following the ministry of a minister in America, Dr Rodney Howard Browne, and then recently we got connected through Twitter. Quite remarkable. My wife sent a tweet to Dr Browne and copied me. It was a bit jokey, about golf. He responded, so I responded to him. Anyway, to cut a long story short, the last time I was in Surrey with my wife we were painting a flat of ours that we're renting out but we were listening to Dr Browne speaking at a meeting which we were streaming on our mobile. The next time I was down another minister friend of mine was opening a brand-new building in Surrey and Dr Browne was there and I met with him. We've become friends. I connected with him and he invited us to Florida for a ministers' and leaders' conference. Isn't that awesome? Isn't God good?

If I'd had the choice to meet anybody in the world, I would have chosen to meet Dr Rodney Howard Browne, whom I've got to know as one of the the most loving, humble and generous people I've met in my

There's another Greek word: *exousia*. *Exousia* means authority, influence. God is raising this church up to be a dynamic, authoritative, influential voice in this community and beyond.

You might say, 'But I've got no authority.' Yes, you do. You have authoritative, influential power. I believe God's raising the church up and that means raising us up as individuals within our workplaces, within our universities, within our families, within our communities, within this nation.

Hebrews 11:6 says, 'Without faith it is impossible to please [God] . . . he is a rewarder of them that diligently seek him.' That's what you're doing in this season. This is an encouragement to keep on keeping on. Keep on doing that. You see some Christians – we call them the 'Misraelites', not the Israelites. As someone once said, if you can't wake up with a smile, go to a bed with a coat hanger in your mouth! Please don't go and tell anybody about Jesus with a miserable face, you'll scare them. We should have joy unspeakable and be full of glory.

The power of God will break you out of being miserable. The definition of power is 'the ability or capacity to perform or act effectively; strength or force, exerted or capable of being exerted; might, the ability or official capacity to exercise control'. God is increasing our power, let's not deny it. Forcefulness, effectiveness, a noble or unusual power. People should say about us, 'There's something different about this person. There's something noble about them. Why are they always happy?' People say it about me everywhere we go. People say I'm unusual, I'm unique. But we're all unique. The difference is the anointing. It's the power of God. Don't deny the power – please accept it.

CHAPTER FOUR

HOW DO WE DENY THE POWER

W hen we look for excuses for our actions or the way we live our lives, we are denying the power of God. We deny the power when we look to blame others: 'But you don't know about my wife', 'You don't know about my husband', 'You don't know about my family, my community', 'I was dropped on my head as a baby'! How long ago was that? Sixty-two years, come on. Yes, things do happen but let's not make excuses. Let's live in *exousia*, not excuse ya!

How do we deny the power? We live in virtual reality. There's a church movement that I'm involved in who use words like, 'Oh we're passionate and intentional.' 'We're missional.' You may be passionate, intentional and missional, but when was the last time you told somebody about Jesus? We can get lost in 'Christianese', in all the jargon. Let's not get lost in virtual reality, having a form of godliness but denying the power. We need to pray that a new power is released in our lives, that old powers will be broken.

An outward working of this power is a mobilisation into evangelism. You'll become more good news. You'll share the good news. Once we start sharing the gospel with other people we're reaffirming and reiterating it in and through our own lives.

We deny the power when we have a victim mentality: 'Oh, poor me. Oh why me? If only you knew. Somebody hurt me in church.' We sometimes hold on for years to things that have hurt us in the past. Come on, let's forgive and bless and walk in love and move on. Don't deny the power of walking in love.

We deny the power when we have a 'can't do' mentality: 'Oh I can't do that, I couldn't possibly.' Now maybe you couldn't, but maybe you and God makes a majority and you could. In Jesus' name we have power. Maybe you could go for that job. Maybe you could reach out to that community. Maybe you could start doing that level of qualification. You and God form a majority. Don't deny the power.

We deny the power when we become lazy. We can become lazy and justify it to ourselves. We can stay put or go backwards even. The truth of the matter is we've got to keep leaning into God, relying on his power to fail forwards into the mercy of God.

The Bible tells us in 1 John 1:9, 'If we confess our sin, he is faithful and just to forgive us our sins, and to cleanse us from all unrighteousness.' Why do we accept the power? We take responsibility. We stop blaming other people. We take full responsibility.

Corrie ten Boom, a survivor of the Nazi concentration camps in World War II who became an incredible evangelist, said, 'God forgives our sin but he cannot forgive our excuses.' Let's stop taking our excuses to God. Let's stop taking the reasons we fail to God. If we confess our sin he's faithful. He cleanses us. Fail forward to the mercy of God.

The blood of Jesus hasn't lost any of its power. Not just to forgive you from sin but to deliver you from sin, to walk holy and pure, and true. A holy life is a powerful life.

Don't deny the power of healing. In Isaiah it says, 'With his stripes we are healed.' In the Living Bible, Malachi 4:2 says, 'For you who fear my name, the Sun of Righteousness will rise with healing in his wings. And you will go free, leaping with joy like calves let out to pasture.' Don't deny the power of God's healing. God's healing power will move in your lives today for some of you; other's you're going to have to keep contending, believing the Word of God, pressing on in prayer. Pressing in, pressing on, calling higher. Don't deny the power.

Don't deny the power of God's provision and 'my God shall supply all your needs according to his riches in glory by Christ Jesus' (Philippians 4:19). It's a done deal. It's interesting that this scripture comes on the back of Paul sharing with the church about giving, and being generous and sowing. A Bible-based church will believe in tithes and offerings and giving.

About twenty years ago Jill and I were in a church that had nothing. We took offerings. We were praying all the time, fasting, praying, reaching out, and we became a very generous church and kept giving and sowing.

accursed, and no one can say that Jesus is Lord except by the Holy Spirit. There are diversities of gifts, but the same Spirit. There are differences of ministries, but the same Lord. And there are diversities of activities, but it is the same God who works all in all. But the manifestation of the Spirit is given to each one for the profit of all: for to one is given the word of wisdom through the Spirit, to another the word of knowledge through the same Spirit, to another faith by the same Spirit, to another gifts of healings by the same Spirit, to another the working of miracles, to another prophecy, to another discerning of spirits, to another different kinds of tongues, to another the interpretation of tongues. But one and the same Spirit works all these things, distributing to each one individually as He wills. (NKJV)

As I read this I can feel the anointing. I can feel the power of God. When we speak about the person of the Holy Spirit, he's very apt to make his presence felt. He's here all the time, but you honour him and you speak about him, and he'll turn up. Why? To glorify Jesus, that's what he does, and he's God Almighty. He's not a dove. He's like a dove but he's not a dove. He's not a mighty rushing wind. He's like a mighty rushing – He's God Almighty. Powerful, and he's given us these gifts to get the job done.

THE GIFTS OF TONGUES AND INTERPRETATION

I just want us to look first at the gifts of tongues and interpretation, and I'm going to look back on why I got saved. Somebody led me to Christ in the back streets of Manchester when I was twenty-one. I was involved in drugs, gangs and crime. I was a total mess; I was the neighbourhood crazy guy. My girlfriend worked in a bank . . . you can imagine what that led to. An evangelist used to speak to us and tell us, 'God loves you, Jesus died for you, and he's got a plan for your life.' That's it. That's the gospel, isn't it? My friends would try to make fun of him, and I'd say no, because he was bold. He had the power of God on him. You could see it in his eyes, and you could feel love coming from him in sincerity. So I said, 'No, listen to this guy.'

One night, some crazy stuff was going on and we went to him.

He invited us in and said, 'You're playing in the devil's playground. God loves you. Jesus died for you. He's got a plan for your life. Give your life to Christ.' We got down on our knees and gave our lives to Christ. As I said earlier, I knew what *I'd* done, but I didn't know what *he'd* done. There are many Christians today who are living like that. They know what they've done, but they don't really know what he's done. Eight years later, after nearly dying four times, after being in nearly every prison in the UK, I'd given my life to Christ, but the Lord started drawing me through the book of Matthew and the teachings of Jesus. I was becoming attracted to the person of Jesus Christ.

> *Do not worry about your life, what you will eat or what you will drink; nor about your body, what you will put on. Is not life more than food and the body more than clothing? Look at the birds of the air, for they neither sow nor reap nor gather into barns; yet your heavenly Father feeds them . . . So why do you worry about clothing? Consider the lilies of the field, how they grow: they neither toil nor spin.* (Matthew 6:25–29 NKJV)

I thought, wow, this is amazing. My friend and I read 1 Corinthians 12, and the next night we read 1 Corinthians 13 (it's the next chapter; you would do, wouldn't you?). 'Though I speak in the tongues of men and of angels, but have not love . . .' There you go.

I might have the gift of prophecy, I might understand all the mysteries, I might have all the faith to move mountains, but if I don't have love, I am nothing.

Then I said to my friend, 'What's this "tongues" here? It says it here and it says it the chapter before? What is it?' And suddenly, he received the gift of tongues and started speaking in a language we didn't know.

I got the gift of interpretation. How can I describe it? I've never had the gift of interpretation since but my friend spoke in a different language and then, in the middle of that, it translated to English, and this is what the Holy Spirit said to me: 'Jesus died so that your sin can be forgiven.' I'd heard it thousands of times. I'd seen it on posters. But that day the Holy Spirit spoke it to me. The power of God. I knew that I knew that I knew that Jesus had died for me! The whole room lit up, waves and waves of the anointing of the glory of God just started coursing through my body, and I was weeping like a baby because I knew that I knew that I knew that Jesus died for me. The old Pentecostal 'assurance of salvation' – I knew that I knew that I knew that God loved me, Jesus died for me, and he's got a plan for my life. Thank God for the person of the Holy Spirit. Thank God for his gifts.

THE GIFT OF DISCERNING SPIRITS

I've already mentioned how, many years before I gave my life to Christ, I'd been into a lot of crazy stuff. On one occasion we'd been taking drugs and a friend of mine was reading this witchcraft book with all these spells and stuff.

I got the gift of discerning of spirits. It was like the curtains pulled back and I could see into another realm. I saw these demonic beings fall into the room and fall on my friends. They looked like huge frogs and were all misshapen. It mentions it in the book of Revelation. Read it and you'll see. They were like big frogs, huge frogs. I've seen it since. I thought *Wow!* It totally freaked me out. At that time nothing scared me. I'd fight van-loads of police, doormen – I wasn't scared of anybody, I'd just fight them – but this freaked me out. It led to my salvation.

The discerning of spirits is very real, and can happen. You can go into a room and you can feel an evil spirit, you can feel a bad presence, can't you? You can sense if there is something about a person's spirit you don't like. Discerning the spirits. God will protect you and God will lead you through the gifting of the Holy Spirit.

THE GIFT OF FAITH

The mighty, awesome gift of faith. Somebody once said that it's like God's supernatural power and gift to get the job done. It's like he unscrews your head and pours in pure nitrogen. It's like an awesome gift where you know that you know that you know that God has spoken and this thing is going to come to pass. 'Faith comes by hearing, and hearing by the word of God' (Romans 10:17 NKJV). I'm sure you know that by now. The Bible tells us in Galatians 5:22–23 that faith is a fruit of the Spirit. I'll tell you, don't deny the power of the mighty gift of faith.

If you've got all these three kicking together, it's totally awesome. You become like Abraham: you become fully persuaded.

The gift of faith isn't just for in a meeting or church service. Anybody with a broken back can be totally healed through the power of God. I've seen the gift of faith operate like that. The mighty gift of faith can apply to your personal lives in a practical way – in your family, in your career, in your call, in your vocation. Are you excited about that?

I'm going to give you some examples from my life. When I lived in Sheffield, even as a Christian I was struggling with anger. I was struggling with anger and jealousy so much that I smashed up a wardrobe with my bare hands. Then I felt really guilty, as you do when you do stuff you don't want to do, and I cried out to God. Then I read James 5:15–16:

And the prayer offered in faith will make the sick person well; the Lord will raise them up. If they have sinned, they will be forgiven. Therefore confess your sins to each other and pray for each other so that you may be healed. The prayer of a righteous person is powerful and effective.

When I read this I was in a place of total brokenness. I'd just done something really crazy and blown it. But I cried out to God, and I read this and it jumped off the page at me. God spoke to me and suddenly I had faith that I was going to be healed. I got the gift of faith. Me, personally. I was totally, fully persuaded that I was going to be healed.

What did I do next? I called my pastor. The Bible says that we should call to the elders of the church and they'll anoint us with oil, pray for the sick, raise us up. I called my pastor.

We should have answer phones for the church phones to make it easier: 'Thank you for phoning the office of the pastor. If you'd like to confess your sin, just listen to the following instructions. For the lost, press one. For anger, press two. For drug problems, press the hashtag. For gossip, phone a friend . . .'

that's OK. God's big enough to hear that. If I'm disappointed about something in my heart, I shouldn't just cover it up because if I hide that feeling I'll become a total fake. I'll have nobody to communicate to me heart to heart because I'll be living a total lie. You can say many things about me but I'm a WYSIWYG. Hannah in the story was a WYSIWYG: what you see is what you get. God loves everybody, but there's something about being a WYSIWYG where God will not deny the power of your prayer.

In the Scripture passage we are told that this man Elkanah went up from his city yearly to worship and sacrifice to the Lord of Hosts in Shiloh. The two sons of Eli, the priests of the Lord, were there. When it came time to give offerings, he would give portions to his wives and daughters, and he'd give Hannah double. There are some people that go to church and they pay up their offerings. They do the religious duties. They go to church. They lift their hands – maybe, maybe not. They say hello. They do whatever. They go to church on a Sunday or a Wednesday night and maybe to a conference. I would say that is religion. This guy, Hannah's husband, was paying his religious duties. We can go to church Sunday morning. We can go to house group Wednesday. We can go to this conference or that conference, but what about every other day? What about Monday, Tuesday, Thursday, Friday? What about those days? Hannah's husband didn't really need to be like Hannah because he was totally satisfied. He was totally happy. He'd got two beautiful wives and he's got children. He's happy. Nothing wrong with him.

Hannah is deeply disappointed, isn't she? She's provoked. That's a good thing. It's important to address disappointment and let it come to the surface. We shouldn't mask things. We can put layers on and keep our jealousy and disappointment inside of us. Hannah let it all out.

Then Elkanah her husband said to her, 'Hannah, why do you weep? Why do you not eat? And why is your heart grieved? Am I not better to you than ten sons?'

I mean, who does he think he is? God's gift to women? He thinks he is, doesn't he? 'Poor Hannah,' he's saying to her, 'why do you need all that? I'm totally enough for you. Can't I satisfy your every desire?' Well, no. You can't satisfy my every desire. 'Am I not better to you than ten sons?' No, you're not.

Hannah didn't even dignify it with a response.

So Hannah arose after they had finished eating and drinking in Shiloh. Now Eli the priest was sitting on the seat by the doorpost of the tabernacle of the LORD. And she was in bitterness of soul, and prayed to the LORD and wept in anguish.

She was pretty serious, wasn't she? She was in bitterness of soul, and praying to the Lord, and weeping in anguish. I imagine it sounds like a cat being strangled. That's all I can think of about bitterness of soul.

Then she made a vow . . .

This is where it gets serious.

. . . and said, 'O LORD of hosts, if You will indeed look on the affliction of Your maidservant and remember me, and not forget Your maidservant, but will give Your maidservant a male child, then I will give him to the LORD all the days of his life, and no razor shall come upon his head.' And it happened, as she continued praying before the LORD, that Eli watched her mouth. Now Hannah spoke in her heart; only her lips moved, but her voice was not heard. Therefore Eli thought she was drunk. So Eli said to her, 'How long will you be drunk? Put your wine away from you!'

She's got anguish of soul. She's pouring her heart out to the Lord. Now she's praying, probably lost her voice, totally at the end itself, and now, on top of everything, the pastor accuses her of being drunk! It's going from bad to worse for Hannah.

But Hannah answered and said, 'No, my lord, I am a woman of sorrowful spirit. I have drunk neither wine nor intoxicating drink, but have poured out my soul before the LORD. Do not consider your maidservant a wicked woman, for out of the abundance of my complaint and grief I have spoken until now.' Then Eli answered and said, 'Go in peace, and the God of Israel grant your petition which you have asked of Him.' And she said, 'Let your maidservant find favour in your sight.' So the woman went her way and ate, and her face was no longer sad.

I find it amazing. Look at what she's done. She's been crying, screaming, grieving. Then she lost her breath. She's lost her voice and it seemed like she lost her mind! The priest accuses her of being drunk. She explains the situation. Then suddenly he says, 'Go in peace, and the God of Israel grant your petition which you have asked of him.' This is very powerful. When he said, 'Go in peace,' that word 'peace' means *shalom* peace: nothing missing, nothing broken. 'The Lord grant your request.' She went away in total peace, and she wasn't sad.

It was like Eli the priest spoke a prophetic word over her life. She got the gift of faith. She had total peace. She knew that she knew that she knew that she was going to have a child. She wasn't sad anymore.

I've experienced this many, many times. I've got very serious and said, 'God, this is how I feel. I'm sick and tired. I've had enough of this. You're meant to be a loving God. I'm meant to have this. I haven't got it. I've had enough.' Then suddenly I've felt the peace of God. I've no longer been sad. I've gone away, like Hannah did, and I knew that I knew that I knew that my request had been granted by the Lord.

I remember when I was in total drug addiction. Totally down. I couldn't get up in the morning if I didn't score drugs. I couldn't sleep at night if I didn't score drugs. All my money, all my life, was consumed by my drug addiction. I needed that chain broken. On one beautiful day, through the power of the name of Jesus and prayer, the power of God touched me and I was set free in peace; *shalom*, go your own way. I'm not sad anymore. God answered me.

At one point in my life I needed a job. I was provoked to jealousy, like Hannah, because other people had jobs. They were all happy families. I said, 'Well, God, I've got no job and I need a job.' I prayed in anguish. I was honest with the Lord, like Hannah was. That request was made. Somebody prayed for me. I felt the peace of God, and I knew that I knew that I knew that I would have a job. It's called the gift of faith.

It happened to me when I was leading a big organisation and I prayed and prayed and prayed and cried my heart out to God about provision. Suddenly I found the peace of God. It happens on the inside first; then you see it on the outside.

I prayed about a wife for years and years. I was single for so, so long. All my friends were getting married but I was alone. I was happy, but it was provoking jealousy in me. I had a nice life but I prayed and prayed. I felt like the loneliest man in the world. I remember walking on the beach one day and I cried to God with anguish and bitterness of soul. I always feel the Lord comfort me. I felt the Lord promise me a wife who would be the same as me. We'd come together. We'd do a great work for God.

When Jill and I started falling in love, again I prayed to the Lord, 'Is this right? Is this what you want, Lord?' A friend of mine came around to my place, just catching up. At the end, we had a prayer time with each other. As we prayed he started thanking God for my wife. I hadn't told him anything. As he was thanking God for my wife, I just started weeping over the anointing, the presence of God. I had peace. I was no longer sad. I knew that Jill was going to be my wife.

I say the Lord speaks to me. He'll speak to you the same. We should get very real before God and make our requests known to God. Is there something that's provoking us? Is something provoking us to jealousy? What is God's plan for our lives? If there's something on our hearts we should tell God about it. We need to be honest and true.

We all need healing. We all need God to do something in our lives. That thing that is so deep down in our heart no one else knows about – the Lord knows. He wants to touch you. He wants to heal you. I believe God wants to give us the desires of our hearts. There are certain things in your heart and in your life that you still want, that you still feel haven't happened to you. God loves you, and he wants to give to you.

I don't know what it might be. It might be a child like Hannah. It might be a loving caring husband. God will provide. God has a great plan for you. He really has.

THE DESPERATE FATHER

Now when Jesus had crossed over again by boat to the other side, a great multitude gathered to Him; and He was by the sea. And behold, one of the rulers of the synagogue came, Jairus by name. And when he saw Him, he fell at His feet and begged Him

Here's another occasion where Jesus goes to preach to the multitudes and the crowds are pressing in on him. He saw two blokes standing by the lake washing their nets and he just sat in Simon Peter's boat and asked him to push away from the land so that he could carry on teaching without being swamped by the crowds of people. Simon Peter had been fishing all night and caught nothing. He was exhausted, tired, burned out. He'd worked all night and had nothing to show for it. He had made no money for his family, for the mortgage, no money for the kids, no nothing. Jesus came to him, asking if he could use the boat. 'Can I borrow your business, bro?' 'Yeah, Jesus. I don't really need it. The fish ain't biting, you know what I mean?'

Any of us who are building businesses, if we give them to the Lord he will bless them. Simon Peter gave his business to Jesus. It's his boat, it's his business. Jesus finishes speaking and then says to Simon Peter and he says, 'Bro, just cast on the other side.' Peter thinks, 'What is this guy about? He's a carpenter. I'm a fisherman. The fish only bite in the shallow. He's telling me to go in the deep. Well, either way, I'm going to go.'

He'd been around Jesus, he knew what he was talking about. He fished in the deep. Maybe God was showing him, and maybe showing us that we should not limit ourselves to fishing in the shallows. Small dreams. Small Bible study. Small prayers: 'Oh, bless the Lord, bless the bees, bless the trees. Oh Lord, bless our conflicts today,' or whatever. Do you know what I mean? Maybe Jesus was saying, 'OK, how deep do you want to go?' Fish in the deep, get out in the deep. Get out of the shallow relationship that's pulling you down. If we leave those people behind, where are we going to go, who'll be with us? Sometimes desperate faith breaks you all up. I'll tell you right now, when we choose to walk a life of loneliness with God, he will meet us in his divine power, and he'll make a divine strategic partnership. When Peter fished in the deep he had his biggest catch of fish ever. Biggest. You can say biggest business transaction, biggest coin trust, biggest finance. As he's pulling in the haul, he signals to his friends in the other boats and they come and help him. Together. He went from being alone, fishing like an idiot, catching nothing, to obeying Jesus' words through the power of desperation, and he had a huge catch of fish, with new divine strategic partners.

HOW DESPERATE ARE YOU

Don't deny the power of desperation. We all get desperate. How desperate are you? How hungry are you for change? How desperate are you for breakthrough in your life? How desperate are you to break through in your own family? In your own ministry? You've got to keep pushing and pushing. Imagine the woman in the story. She's got to get through thousands upon thousands of people. Not one, two, ten, a hundred, but a thousand. Don't deny the power of desperation, because as she's pushing through and pushing through – suddenly – she touched him. And she didn't even have to touch *him*, just the hem of his garments, and there was so much power flowing out of him that she was totally healed. 'And Jesus, immediately knowing in Himself that power had gone out of Him, turned around in the crowd and said, "Who touched My clothes?"'

See, the power that went out of Jesus there is the same as the power in Acts 1:8: 'You will receive power when the Holy Spirit comes on you; and you will be my witnesses in Jerusalem, and in all Judea and Samaria, and to the ends of the earth.' I'll tell you, to be an effective witness you need to do it under *dunamis* power. Really. Otherwise, you're a clanging gong or a clanging cymbal and there's no anointing. Get desperate before God, and you shall receive power – *dunamis* power, dynamite, Holy Ghost power.

Jill and I were in Florida at the ministers and leaders conference and went to some mighty meetings. We were driving back from Tampa, Florida, to the Gulf of Mexico to stay in a place called Madeira Beach. We stopped off at a pancake house to eat and got talking with the waitress there. 'What do you do?' she asked.

'I'm glad you asked. We're missionaries. We tell people God loves them and that Jesus died for them. Do you mind if we pray for you?'

We prayed for her and led her to Christ. The power of God hit her and she started weeping under the anointing. She said, 'You don't know how much I needed this. I've been so desperate.' She told me her husband had died the previous year from pneumonia. Her sister is a Christian and had been praying for her. I said, 'The Lord met you in your need.'

Don't deny the power of desperation. Stay desperate. Stay humble.

Don't let the religious coneheads close you down. Don't let people at work shut you down. Don't let people in your family quieten you down. Cry out all the louder.

great rejoicing when people come to you and say, 'I'm so thankful that you shared the gospel with me. I'm so glad.' We're literally going to be snatching people from hell.

He said to them, 'Go into all the world and preach the gospel to all creation. Whoever believes and is baptised will be saved, but whoever does not believe will be condemned.' (Mark 16:15–16)

Jesus is telling us to go and preach the gospel, the good news. Those who believe and receive will be saved; those who don't are dammed already. That's a fact. And the great thing about Jesus is that in everything he asks us to do, he goes with us and he empowers us. By evangelising we're really, really fulfilling the great commission, we're fulfilling God's plan and the prayer of Jesus, so all heaven is behind us and all heaven is literally on our side.

So by evangelising we're doing what Jesus wants us to do. Do you remember the WWJD wristbands? What would Jesus do? Well, this is exactly what he would, and did, do. He came to seek and save the lost, destroy the works of the enemy, and he came that we might have life and have it in all its fullness.

He told them, 'The harvest is plentiful, but the workers are few. Ask the Lord of the harvest, therefore, to send out workers into his harvest field.' (Luke 10:2 NIV)

By evangelising, we're fulfilling the prayer of Jesus and the prayer of the early disciples. What is God's will for my life? This is it. John Wesley said, 'God rewards those who go after souls.' He does. I've always been a soul winner, and God has always rewarded me. Hebrews 11:6 says, 'He who comes to God must believe that He is, and that He is a rewarder of those who diligently seek Him.' We cannot see God more than diligently seeking him for the souls of men and women. Get ready for God openly rewarding you, and continuing to reward you as you win souls.

THE STORY OF THE4POINTS

My name is Dave Sharples and since 1993 I have lived and worked with inner city kids and young people in Liverpool (Toxteth), England. During this time I have tried to help make the Church accessible and relevant to local families by communicating the gospel in a simple and memorable way. I also support local lads and young men to live out their faith through a discipleship programme called Mighty Men. I am married and have three children.

In 1995, my wife and I went to Metro Ministries in New York where we were inspired by the work of Bill Wilson and quickly adopted many principles of their ministry. One of these was a simple way to communicate the essence of the gospel called 'the four most important things in the world!' which is similar to the wordless gospel first used by Spurgeon in 1866 to explain the gospel to inner city orphans in London, and the four spiritual laws tract written by Bill Bright in 1952. We started teaching the four most important things every week but changed the name to the4points to make it simpler. We used verbal repetition and visual illustration to help the kids remember each point.

In 2005 my friend Nick Jillard and I were considering resources for the Kidz Klub national network in the UK and had the idea of creating a graphic logo based on the4points. The concept was to form a cryptic and intriguing mathematical equation that would spark conversations and help people to share their faith. We realised straight away that we had 'almost by accident' created a tool for international evangelism that broke both the literacy and language barriers.

Having spent some time crafting the design of the logo, we wrote and designed the fold out tract, and ordered our first batch of silicone wristbands, which to this day are still the two most popular tools we have produced. The tracts can now be personalised on the back panel, to help with follow up and are available in over twenty languages.

Other resources for mission include balloons, clothing, caps and lanyards. The4points logo has been put on cars, buses, taxis, even a hot air balloon and several music videos! The simplicity of the4points logo makes it very versatile, easy to use and instantly recognisable.

The4points operates as a not-for-profit company promoting and facilitating use of the logo all around the world for personal, local, citywide and national outreach. Partners include independent churches, several major denominations and ministries such as United Christian Broadcasters, One Hope, Luis Palau International, Campus Crusade for Christ, Every Home for Christ, to name a few. Rather than rely on donations, we fund our operation solely through the sale of resources.

Our heart is to facilitate outreach all over the world and we can make the4points logo artwork available on request. If you would like to partner with us or use the4points in any way please do get in touch.

God bless,

'Captain' Dave Sharples MBE

Director THE4POINTS.COM

A heart, a multiplication sign, the cross of Christ and a question mark. There you go. It's the gospel made simple. Can the simple gospel message really change people's lives today? Absolutely. Let's go through it.

God loves me

The first thing you need to know is that God is crazy about you, and it is unconditional. There is nothing you can do that will make God love you any more or any less than he already does right now. There is nothing God wants more than to love and be loved by us.

I have sinned

Sadly we have been separated from God's love by something the Bible calls sin. Simply put, sin is when we do something to please ourselves rather than God. We sin when we ignore God, break his laws and basically do something our own way. Sin destroys relationships with friends, with family and with God. The Bible says that sin, ultimately, brings death. That's a great point, a really, really good point to share with people because the wages of sin is death but the gift of God is eternal life. We all want a free gift, don't we?

Jesus died for me

This is probably one of the most well-known facts in the history of mankind, but is often misunderstood. The key is to realise that the penalty for sin is death. We've all sinned and we all deserve to die. But God, who is full of mercy, loves you so much that he sent Jesus to die in your place. Jesus died so that we can have eternal life. It's a free gift. Not only did Jesus die for our sin, but three days later he rose from the dead. Through his death and resurrection, Jesus made a way for us to have a relationship with God.

I need to decide to live for God

All we need to do is to accept we've sinned, ask for God's forgiveness, and then decide to live the rest of our life for him – the choice is ours.

If someone you're going through the 4points with decides to accept God's forgiveness and live their life for him, you can then pray this simple prayer with them:

Dear God, thank you that you died for me and want the best for me in every situation. I'm sorry for ignoring you and doing things my way. I realise now that my sin has hurt you and the people around me and, for this, I am truly sorry. Thank you, Jesus, that you came and took the punishment for my sin. Thank you that you gave your life for me. Please forgive me and help me now as I decide to live only for you. Amen.

A good 'opener' when evangelising is to offer people a gift – a book or booklet or a CD. This tract is a good gift in itself but we should be doing more than giving out tracts. The way I teach evangelism is that we should talk people through this, but it's really about keeping it simple, the KISS principle: keep it simple sanctified. When sharing your story one-on-one, just be friendly and natural. I think it's very important to show who you are quickly and say, 'Well, actually, I'm a Christian.' Just be bold about it. When I first became a Christian and I was sharing my story, I thought that if people could be bold about supporting Man United or Liverpool or Chelsea or Rotherham United or whoever, if people can be so full-on and keen about football teams, rugby teams and pop groups, then how much more bold should we be when we're on about Jesus, the King of kings, the Lord of lords. He saved us, forgave us and gave us a brand-new life. Not just this life, but for eternity. It's huge! I mean, it's hard to even articulate. Eternity! Life is just a whisper, but if we can live with eternity in mind, we'll live a big life.

It's easier than you imagine to open up a conversation about Jesus. You can simply ask, 'Has anybody ever told you God loves you, Jesus died for you and has a plan for your life? Can I just talk you through this?' Then you can talk them through the script of the4points tract: has anybody told you God loves you; the Bible says we have sinned; Jesus has died for you; we need to decide if we want to live for God or not. It's that simple . . . really that simple. Keep taking them back to the script if they try to take you away by talking about how they used to go to church, or they're a good person or this or that. Take them back to the script then ask if you can pray for them. Most people will say OK. It's not a bad idea to practise this with people in your church. You could meet in small groups and split into pairs to just practise talking through the4points to help you to grow in courage and confidence.

You can use the same principle with your family of course. It's a good principle. I've led my mum and two sisters to the Lord. I'm still going for my two brothers, you know what I mean. But, this is a great tool because it depersonalises it from you; because your family members know you, they know how to navigate and wrestle you. But this is a proven tool – keep taking them back to it.

If anybody you speak to does accept Christ and you pray with them, by all means give them a card inviting them to your church. Or if people can't or don't want to stop and listen whilst you talk them through the4points, give them the tract and a card inviting them to your church. But evangelising isn't about getting people to come to church. What does the Bible say? It doesn't say go and invite people to church. You see, this is simple – it says go and preach the gospel. That's all it says do.

So we're fulfilling the great commission, so we're going to go and share the good news and we're going to lead people to Christ. But I tell you something, when you go and share the good news, you can feel the anointing, because when you share the good news it does *you* more good than *them*. Wow, God loves me, Jesus died for me, he's got a plan for my life! It's reaffirming the gospel in your own life. When you witness to the power of God, the power comes (Acts 1:8). I'm like this all the time! The gospel is the power of God unto salvation. 'First to them who believe.' That's you and me! Everything we need is in the gospel. Isn't that amazing? It's not out there, it's in the gospel and that can be in me, totally whole. Isn't it good news?

As you share your story and as you don't deny your testimony or deny the name of Jesus, God will protect you, provide for you and reward you. My life has proved it. That's one-on-one evangelism.

PUBLIC TESTIMONY

Once you start sharing your story who knows where you'll end up. I started sharing my story in churches and then I'd get invited to businessmen's fellowships to speak. I shared in prisons, businesses, conferences, churches, and then I started to train others in evangelism.

It's just about being faithful in small ways, and God will give you big in anything in life. Just be faithful. Whenever a door opens and you get an opportunity, take it, because God will give you the power. Like I said earlier, he will quicken you to share your story.

A few guidelines when sharing your testimony from a public platform:

Respect and build great relations with the people who are inviting you, and stick to the guidelines and constraints – blessed are the short winded, for they get invited back! If you're asked to speak for 15 minutes, stick to 15 minutes. If you've got half an hour, speak for half an hour.

Prepare by writing a scripture on paper and some 'trigger' phrases, and don't be afraid to use humour. Humour is great for building rapport.

Don't waste any words. Give top-line information. Be very quick.

- Introduce yourself, where you're coming from and that you're going to be sharing a story.

- First point: family history.

- Second point: could be something that happened to you, good or bad, and the effect this had on your life.

- Third point: how you came to learn about and accept the gospel. Always be careful to make the second part of your story as big as, if not bigger, than the first half: 'I'm Terry. I'm lonely. I've been a drug addict. I was an idiot. My body was racked in pain. I've been in every prison in the country. I was involved in serious crime. My life was a mess. I was a write-off, and I became a Christian.' I mean, that's like a lead balloon. 'I found that God loved me. Jesus died for me. Then I found out he healed me. I actually felt the healing power of God when somebody prayed for me. I was healed.' I explain Jesus is my saviour, my healer.

- Fourth point: how God has provided for you and opened doors for you.

Don't underestimate the power of your story, because your story and you sharing the gospel can see people totally come into faith for eternity.

You don't know what people are going through in the audience, because everybody is going through something. If you know God loves you, Jesus died for you and that he's got a plan for your life, part of that plan is to share his gospel with that group of people. It's huge what can be accomplished through your life. You're like a little stick of dynamite in God's hand. When we put what we've got into God's mighty hand, it becomes something huge.

Know your audience. It's always good to do a bit of research. Find out a bit about the church: what their vision is, their mission. What are the needs of your audience? What are they coming up to? What are they doing?

Be yourself. Learn from other people, but don't try to be somebody else. Somebody once said, 'You're born original. Don't die a copy.' We can't be somebody else because that space is already taken. Just let your own light shine. Jesus said, 'Let your light so shine before men, that they may see your good works and glorify your Father in heaven' (Matthew 5:16 NKJV). The most anointed and greatest person you can be is you. That's good, isn't it? That takes the pressure off!

Make people smile. Smiles are great. The face is like the headlights of your heart. The face gives a lot away. As I said before: if you can't wake up with a smile on your face, go to bed with a coat hanger in your mouth. Please, smile. God loves you. Jesus died for you. He's got a plan for your life. Even if you've got one tooth, smile.

Study and learn from others. We have everything at our fingertips: YouTube, Google, podcasts, DVDs, CDs, books – everything's there. Study your Bible. You can get it and listen to it on your phones or tablets. Read other people's testimonies and life stories. Read them and learn from them because you will see that if God can do that for others and through others, then he can do it through you, too.

Pray into and for opportunities. As you get opportunities to speak, pray for the church or the organisation you're going to. Pray for the people. Pray people will get saved when you're there and that they will be touched by the power of God. Pray that God will use you, anoint you. Prayer preparation is as important, if not more so, than written preparation. I'll tell you something right now: God can anoint you in five minutes, ten minutes. He can use you powerfully in just a few minutes as well as he can in half an hour.

'Today in the town of David a Saviour has been born to you;
he is the Messiah, the Lord.' (Luke 2:11)

That's a wonderful promise: the Messiah. There was joyful fulfilment of all the Messiah prophecies that day. The Messiah's here and he's going to deliver his people. He was wounded for our transgressions. He was bruised for our inequities. By his stripes we are healed.

Suddenly a great company of the heavenly host appeared with
the angel, praising God and saying, 'Glory to God in the highest
heaven, and on earth peace to those on whom his favour rests.'
(Luke 2:13–14)

'Suddenly . . .' The Son of the living God has come to us. When we take God seriously, he will take us seriously. Totally. And 'suddenlies' will come. Suddenly a door will open. Suddenly you'll meet this person. Sudden you'll be introduced to that person. Suddenly an opportunity will arise. Suddenly . . .

Peace on earth. Peace means nothing missing, nothing broken. The devil will tell you that you should have this or that, he'll scream at you in the midnight hour, he'll scream at you in the morning: go do this, go do that, go over there, it's never enough. Nothing missing. Nothing broken. *Shalom.* Peace. This isn't the kind of peace you get on a cruise; you can't get it on a holiday. The peace of God transcends all understanding. The peace of God, glory in the highest, peace on earth to those on whom his favour rests.

When the angels had left them and gone into heaven, the
shepherds said to one another, 'Let's go to Bethlehem and see this
thing that has happened, which the Lord has told us about.' So
they hurried off and found Mary and Joseph, and the baby, who
was lying in the manger. When they had seen him, they spread
the word concerning what had been told them about this child,
and all who heard it were amazed at what the shepherds said to
them. (Luke 2:15–18)

Hebrews 11:6 says, 'Without faith it is impossible to please God, because anyone who comes to him must believe that he exists and that he rewards those who earnestly seek him.' He was commanded through the Christmas story and they sought him with great haste and great urgency.

Now after Jesus was born in Bethlehem of Judea in the days of Herod the king, behold, wise men from the East came to Jerusalem, saying, 'Where is He who has been born King of the Jews? For we have seen His star in the East and have come to worship Him.' (Matthew 2:1–2 NKJV)

Wise men and wise women still seek him but his gift is not just for the wise men. It's for us today. God is rewarding those who diligently seek him. Christmas is such a busy season. There is so much to be done in the lead-up with all the expectations and demands on our time but we should not lose sight of the real reason of Christmas or the opportunities to tell others the gospel story. We should make time to seek him, and I believe he's going to reward us as we continue to do so.

When Herod the king heard this, he was troubled, and all Jerusalem with him. And when he had gathered all the chief priests and scribes of the people together, he inquired of them where the Christ was to be born. So they said to him, 'In Bethlehem of Judea, for thus it is written by the prophet:

"But you, Bethlehem, in the land of Judah,
Are not the least among the rulers of Judah;
For out of you shall come a Ruler
Who will shepherd My people Israel."' (Matthew 2:3–6 NKJV)

It doesn't matter how insignificant you might feel. Can you see how Bethlehem was to be called insignificant? Do you remember Gideon, the prophet in the wine press treading the grapes (Judges 6)? God came to him and said, 'The LORD is with you, you mighty man of valour.' But Gideon's like, 'Oh, I'm insignificant, God. I come from an insignificant family, an insignificant place.' But that's where God loves to come – insignificant places. So no matter how we're feeling – we might feel insignificant; we might feel 'oh, what's going good in my life, in my family, in my role' – this is where God comes to us. God is with us and God is for us. That's what Christmas is all about. The people of Bethlehem felt exactly the same, they felt so insignificant, but that's where Christ came. And that's where he comes to: seemingly insignificant places.

> *'But you, Bethlehem, in the land of Judah, are by no means least among the rulers of Judah; for out of you will come a ruler who will shepherd my people Israel.' Then Herod called the Magi secretly and found out from them the exact time the star had appeared. He sent them to Bethlehem and said, 'Go and search carefully for the child. As soon as you find him, report to me, so that I too may go and worship him.'* (Matthew 2:6–8)

Herod didn't really want to worship him; he wanted to kill him. We will face opposition to our mission. In fact, sometimes when I feel opposition, I think 'bring it on' because I know it means I'm doing something right. Not everyone has pure motives. You could be walking through life with seemingly OK people. But Herod seemed the same to the wise men. He was the king! He was totally influential. So we could think oh, this great influential person here wants to know, wants to come and worship, wants to help. But not everybody who says they want to help does want to help. In fact, they might want to actually kill what's in your heart or on your life. Herod wanted to kill the very Christ-child, the Saviour of the world.

> *After they had heard the king, they went on their way, and the star they had seen when it rose went ahead of them until it stopped over the place where the child was. When they saw the star, they were overjoyed.* (Matthew 2:9–10)

Isn't that amazing? How many people do we know who are ecstatic with joy? How many churches do we go in and we think, 'Wow, look at all these people! They're filled with ecstatic joy. Let's go in there.' In fact, I'm going to talk about the Methodists again. The Methodists got criticised for excessive joy. They were too enthusiastic and they were ostracised. We know out of the seven hundred messages John Wesley preached, only six of them were preached within churches. The rest were out in the open air because nobody would have him, because he was full of ecstatic joy.

I know we have challenges. I know we have issues. But deep, ecstatic joy is our portion. The wise men were ecstatic and they'd only seen the star! Just the knowledge that they were going to find Jesus filled them with joy. They'd not even found him yet.

I remember when I was first touched with ecstatic joy in the backstreets of Manchester. For the first time in my life, I knew that I knew that I knew that Jesus had died so that my sin could be forgiven. I knew it. So much so, I wept tears of ecstatic joy. The whole room lit up. I felt alive. I felt on fire. My heart felt strangely warm.

I remember when I got touched with the power of God in Sheffield. I was prayed for and the power of God totally healed me of all the years of drug abuse, all the scars. I felt ecstatic joy.

I felt ecstatic joy when I got touched and I knew I was going to get a job. I felt ecstatic joy when I knew I was going to marry Jill. The Lord blessed me.

An anointing of the Holy Spirit brings ecstatic joy. And he first came when Christ first came to the earth. And the kings who had not yet met him, by just seeing the star and knowing that they were going to meet him, were filled with ecstatic joy. And we need to understand that this is the portion of the Christian.

The Bible tells us in Galatians 5 that the fruit of the Spirit is love, peace, joy. The kingdom of God is peace, joy and righteousness in the Holy Spirit. Joy is our portion. The joy of the Lord is our strength.

Let's look at the words of one of my favourite carols:

In the bleak midwinter, frosty wind made moan,
Earth stood hard as iron, water like a stone;
Snow had fallen, snow on snow, snow on snow,
In the bleak midwinter long ago.
Our God, heaven cannot hold him, nor earth sustain.

Heaven and earth shall flee away when he comes to reign.
In the bleak midwinter a stable place sufficed
The Lord God Almighty, Jesus Christ.
What can I give him, poor as I am?

If I were a shepherd, I would bring a lamb;
If I were a wise man, I would do my part;
Yet what I can I give him: give my heart.

'What can I give him, poor as I am?' It's just like Jesus said, where our treasure is, there our heart is also. So I just want to encourage all of us at Christmas to give the best gift we can back to Jesus.

What can I give him? Give him my heart.

CHAPTER TEN

BEYOND THE OPEN DOOR

---

*I know your works. See, I have set before you an open door, and
no one can shut it; for you have a little strength, have kept My
word, and have not denied My name.* (Revelation 3:8, NKJV)

I mentioned earlier about when I was going through a time of criticism.
And I just kept worshipping and pushing like never before in faith and
prayer. I was listening to a service being streamed live from somewhere
in the world and a worship song I hadn't heard before was playing:

In the things familiar, we find security,
Resisting all the changes, the days and years to bring,
When God decides to lead you through an open door,
Inviting you to holy grounds, you've never known before.

Beyond the open door is a new and fresh anointing,
Hear the spirit calling you to go beyond the open door,
For the Lord will go before you,
into a greater power you've ever known before,
Beyond the open door.

This worship song came on and I started weeping and weeping, and the
glory of God just came right in the room. We don't have to be in church;
sometimes it helps but it can happen anywhere. Waves and waves of the
anointing of God just started flooding my soul. I can feel that same
anointing now, the glory of God cascading through my body.

Later on that night, the Lord woke me up, and I went to my little
study and prepared a message called 'Beyond the Open Door'. It's a
strong revival message, and it's a strong directional message, I'm telling
you right now it will propel you into new dimensions in the power of
God, in the strength of God. 'Beyond the open door, there's a new and

83

fresh anointing, hear the spirit calling, you to go beyond the open door, for the Lord will go before you into a greater power than you've ever known before.' Are we waiting for this door to open? I mean of course the seasons have gone and we wait and we pray but what does Jesus say? 'I know your works. See I have set before you an open door.' I want to decree and declare over all our lives: God has opened a door over us. The enemy of our souls will tell you 'its closed, it's too late, you can't get that job, you can't get this education, you don't deserve a husband like that, you can't live in that neighbourhood, you can't reach those goals, you can't drive that kind of car'. Oh really? 'I have set before you an open door and nobody can shut it.' Beyond the open door. Well, Pastor, people are talking about me, they're lying about me, they don't really like me, and they'll never open the door.' Well thank God! Thank God it's not man or woman holding the door open for our lives because people are fickle. Your pastor's certainly not fickle, he's the same yesterday, today and forever more. Hebrews 13:8 . . . oh, that's Jesus . . . but he's alive in you, isn't he? A pastor in one of the churches I was in once said to me, 'How you doing, Terry?' I said 'I'm great. I'm the same today, yesterday and forever more. I'm Hebrews 13:8.' *The Message* translation says, 'There should be a consistency that runs through us all. For Jesus doesn't change – yesterday, today, tomorrow, he's always totally himself.' So I am the same yesterday, today and forever more, aren't you?

Listen to this, 'I set before you an open door and no one can shut it; for you have a little strength.' We don't need to be strong, we don't need to have it all together. A little strength, that's all you need. The Lord is looking for people to guide who've got little strength. Lord, I need your help. Please help me. Give me strength, take me beyond the open door.

Second qualification, you 'have kept My word'. The Word of God is sharper than a two-edged sword; it's powerful. He took somebody from the backstreets of Manchester, who'd been totally written off, and he saved me, healed me and I got a hold of God and he got a hold of me and he's done incredible things in my life. Keep the word of God.

Third qualification, 'and have not denied My name'. Don't deny the name of Jesus. If you don't deny him he won't deny you before the Father. We can't be in the closet with our faith. I'm a Christian, I believe

CHAPTER ELEVEN

IT'S ALL WORKING OUT

Can you imagine if we lived our lives like the title of this chapter? How's it going, Terry? It's all working out. How's your marriage, Terry? It's all working out. Your family? Working out. Finance? Working out. Career, ministry? It's all working out. Can you imagine if you could live like this? Isn't it powerful?

I love the book of Romans. Martin Luther was actually converted while reading the introduction to the book of Romans; his heart was strangely warmed. It's a remarkable book. Historians and commentators believe that Romans chapter 8 is the pinnacle, the summit of God's teaching.

> *Likewise the Spirit also helps in our weaknesses. For we do not know what we should pray for as we ought, but the Spirit Himself makes intercession for us with groanings which cannot be uttered. Now He who searches the hearts knows what the mind of the Spirit is, because He makes intercession for the saints according to the will of God. And we know that all things work together for good to those who love God, to those who are the called according to His purpose. For whom He foreknew, He also predestined to be conformed to the image of His Son, that He might be the firstborn among many brethren. Moreover whom He predestined, these He also called; whom He called, these He also justified; and whom He justified, these He also glorified. What then shall we say to these things? If God is for us, who can be against us? He who did not spare His own Son, but delivered Him up for us all, how shall He not with Him also freely give us all things? Who shall bring a charge against God's elect? It is God who justifies. Who is he who condemns? It is Christ who died, and furthermore is also risen, who is even at the right hand of God, who also makes intercession for us.* (Romans 8:26–34 NKJV)

Paul is actually encouraging us that we can live our lives like that. What a thought, what a way to live; talk about a positive motivational lifestyle. It's all working out. Paul goes on to say:

I am persuaded that neither death nor life, nor angels nor principalities nor powers, nor things present nor things to come, nor height nor depth, nor any other created thing, shall be able to separate us from the love of God which is in Christ Jesus our Lord. (Romans 8:38–39 NKJV)

I'm not saying to you today that I know it's all working out for me. That would be great for me, wouldn't it, but it really wouldn't help you. Paul is telling the Romans and the church across time and history. I want the Word of God to touch you and the Spirit of God to drop in you and we will all know together that it's all working out; that all things are working out together for good. Not some things but 'all things'. All things are working out for good in my life, the bad in my life, and even the ugly in my life. The fairy-tale comes to mind: even having the ugly sisters worked out for the good for Cinderella! It actually makes the story. So what if the ugly things, the bad things in our lives at the moment could actually be working together for our good?

I'm reminded of Corrie ten Boom and her family. They were an amazing Christian family who hid Jews in their home during the Second World War. They were captured and eventually placed in a Nazi concentration camp. Corrie was imprisoned with her sister Betsie who was one of those enthusiastic Christians who can sometimes get up your nose or under your skin. So they're in a cell together and Corrie says to her, 'Betsie, what are we going to do now?' Betsie said, 'Well at least we're together, and at least we have a bed.' Corrie said, 'But the bed is full of bedbugs and fleas.' And Betsie said, 'The Bible says that we should pray without ceasing and give thanks in all circumstances, for this is God's will for us. So let's stand here and give thanks.' Corrie asked what they should be giving thanks for. Betsie replied, 'For each other, for the straw bed and for the bedbugs.' So they did.

Betsie died in the concentration camp. Through a 'clerical error' Corrie was released and went on to become one of the greatest evangelists of all time. But listen to this about the good, the bad and the ugly: Corrie found out that nearly all the women in that concentration camp had been raped or badly abused by the guards except Corrie and her sister. Do you know why? The guards wouldn't go near them because of the lice, the fleas and the bedbugs.

Now I think you know what I'm getting at with this, don't you? I'm not talking about us giving thanks for real bedbugs now, but what about those difficult circumstances or those people who irritate us, they feel like bedbugs. Or is that just me who has one or two of those bedbugs? Well maybe those bedbugs are protecting you from something. Look what they protected Corrie from. And we know that all things – the good, the bad and the ugly – are working out together for good. Isn't that phenomenal?

Corrie used to use a marvellous illustration. She spoke of our lives being like a tapestry: on the front, the part that's shown to everyone, you create a beautiful picture. But on the back, the bit that no one except the creator sees, it looks a total mess. She used to talk about how sometimes our lives feel like this: we may feel that things are a mess, like the back of the tapestry, but when you turn it around you'll see that God is doing something very beautiful with our lives.

In all things it's all working out. But it comes with a challenge to those who love God. So it's conditional. It's a prerequisite. A prerequisite to a promise. If you do this, God will do that. If you forgive, you are forgiven. If you give, it's given unto you. If you praise him, the Almighty comes down and inhabits the praise of his people. So for those who love God, it's all working out.

How much do we love God? Do I love my wife Jill? Yes. Do I put her before myself? Yes. Do I honour her? Yes. Do I do nice things for her? Yes. Do I do what she asks me to do? Yes. So, if I put my wife before myself, then my marriage is all working out. If I don't, if I put myself first, I've got a pretty dodgy marriage, and it might not all be working out, in fact it could be working in. That's how it starts. Instead of working out, looking at how we can affect others' lives, we're facing in and only focusing on ourselves. And we know it's all working out to those who love God and put him first. Does Jill put me before herself? Yes, it's all working out. We've got an outward facing life. If you look at my Instagram, it says 'outward facing and serving evangelist' – isn't that good? Some people face outwards not really doing much, but if you're facing and serving, that's good isn't it? It's working out, and we know it's all working out to those who love God and put him first.

Those who have been called, have been called into his purpose. One day when I was sitting in my office, I got a phone call. When I answered the person at the other end said, 'Hello, this is the PA to the Lord Lieutenant of Surrey. I'm just ringing to give you a special invitation to the Queen's garden party.' I was waiting for the punch line, for one of my friends to say 'got you'! But then they asked for my details for security clearance and it was actually true! My spiritual mother at the time was Jill's natural mother; she said Jill might like to come with me, so she got a special letter like I did. We were called by the Queen to go to the garden party. It was very nice. There was a band playing, nice food. Everybody had done nice things in the community. My favourite thing was these little chocolate cakes with the Queen's crest on top with a crown on. If I hadn't have been saved I might've put one in my pocket to take home.

I got a call from the Queen and I felt special. But we get a call from the King of kings and the Lord of lords. And, one day, every tongue will confess, whether they like it or not, that Jesus is Lord to the glory of God the Father. Every queen, every king will lay their crowns at his feet. If we love God first and we're called, we can confidently say and know that it's all working out. Those who've been 'called according to his purpose'. That's the challenge of it, isn't it? It's not oh God can you bless me in this and that and do this and I've prayed. God said it's all working out, put him first, it's working out according to his purpose, God has got a purpose for your life. It's much easier when we yield to that purpose than trying to get our purpose. Bono once said, 'I don't want to ask God to bless what I'm doing, it's probably better if I get what God's doing because that's already blessed.'

What is the rest of his purpose for your life? I don't know. But he does, and he'll tell you. If you truly surrender your dreams, hopes and desires to him, he'll do something with your life, like you couldn't even dream or imagine. It'll be above all that you can ask, imagine, dream of, according to his power at work within you. His power to do his will is mighty, we can say it's all working out.

'Moreover whom He predestined, these He also called.' That's totally huge. Other scriptures also tell us before we were even born God had a plan for our lives:

> *Your eyes saw my unformed body; all the days ordained for me were written in your book before one of them came to be.*
> (Psalm 139:16)

He knows our days, I was meant to be here and so were you, in the plan of God before the foundation of the world. Are we called? Are we going according to his will? Predestination. And this is where it all gets a bit ouch really, because it's all working out, beyond the thing that works in, *'He also predestined to be conformed to the image of His Son.'* Now that's great, we want to be more like Jesus. But Jesus died on the cross. People would put you on a cross. You may get persecution, you may get people coming against you, you may get circumstances coming against you, but if you appeal to his will, his power, Jesus will become big on the inside of you. It's the redemptive purpose of God, working in our lives, through our character. And it all works together for good.

Jill says when she first met me I was a bit of a rough diamond. I was a rough diamond but how do you think I became a polished diamond. It's like the pearl, how is the pearl made? Bit of grit, few bedbugs, knock off the rough edges. Sometimes when we're praying for God to get rid of these people in our lives who get under our skin, or get us out of the circumstances that irritate, God actually wants to mould us and shape us and conform us to the image of his Son. If you've got that mind-set and that understanding, you'll know that it's all working out. Isn't that good? God's beautiful and redemptive plan, allowing us the privilege of becoming more like Jesus. The character of Christ flowing through us, making us sweet, getting rid of the bitterness, the insecurities, the pains, the hurts, the depressions, the oppressions, the love of Christ is living in me. Wow. What a privilege.

There was an evangelist who went to outreach the Native Americans and saw many come to Christ and be touched with the power of God. He was preaching away, preaching away, and there was a Chief with a big headdress on. Nothing happening, no reaction, he's just staring at him. The evangelist said, 'What's wrong?' The Chief said, 'I've heard you talk about small Holy Ghost or big Holy Ghost. We want big Holy Ghost.'

'*Conformed to the image of His Son.*' Conformed to be the image of Christ. How much of his light have we got coming out of us, how much purity? Are we doing things we shouldn't be doing, saying things we shouldn't be saying? Do we know we're missing the mark yet staying in that? Today is the time to just get out of that stuff and let Jesus be formed, big and powerful, on the inside of us.

'*Moreover, those he called*' – the King of kings is calling you right now personally, the Creator of heaven and earth is calling you. '*Whom He called, these He also justified.*' That means that it will be as if I never sinned, just as if I never did any wrong at all; clean, totally pure, holy, faultless, righteous. That's what Jesus did on the cross: he died that I might be justified, that we might be the righteousness of God. If you don't know you're justified, it won't be working out. Think about it. We don't even have the thought or the inclination that it's all working out because we're bound in guilt, shame, in things we've been involved in that we know we shouldn't be. It's so important to know we are justified. Those he justified he also glorified. This is like going from glory to glory to glory. God has glorified us. He's changing us from one level of glory to the next. As we behold him, our lives change from one level of glory to the next. In my Christian walk, I've always gone from one level of glory to the next level of glory but there's always been a gory in between. People have let me down or I've gone through some huge challenges and I've had to let Christ grow bigger on the inside of me through forgiving, through letting some things go. But suddenly I've had another level, and I know it's all working out.

It's a great thought, a great way to live, but it is also a challenge. Is God number one in our lives? If he is we can fully say we know it's all working out. God is calling us today, he's calling us deeper with him. He's calling us deeper in the ministry. He's justified us, just as if we'd never sinned. Are there things in our lives that shouldn't be in our lives? Are we doing things we shouldn't be? Do we need to make God number one?

We know that all things work together for good to those who love God, to those who are the called according to His purpose . . . neither death nor life, nor angels nor principalities nor powers, nor things present nor things to come, nor height nor depth, nor any other created thing, shall be able to separate us from the love of God which is in Christ Jesus our Lord.

'Terry, I need some shining stars in my black holes.' So do I. Black holes to shining stars. The simple message of the gospel.

Now I'm telling you this for a reason. I would not be where I am today if it was not for this message. You don't realise the enormity of what I'm saying, and I'm not looking for congratulations, but the Terry Eckersley of fifteen years ago isn't the Terry Eckersley you see today. Of course the message of the gospel has changed my life forever. If you do not respond to this message, you will not fulfil your full potential in God. I'm telling you right now because I've been around for a long time and I know that if you do not get these black holes sorted in your life, they will sort you.

I'm not the same person I was before because I let the Lord deal with some deep fissures in my soul. As it tells us in 2 Corinthians 5:21, 'God made him who had no sin to be sin for us, so that in him we might become the righteousness of God' and in Colossians 2:14, 'having cancelled the charge of our legal indebtedness, which stood against us and condemned us; he has taken it away, nailing it to the cross'. And I'm urging you, I'm begging you by the mercy of God, to allow the Lord to identify some stuff for you, and respond. And the Lord's going to heal it, in a deep way: 'by his wounds you have been healed' (1 Peter 2:24). Giving up these things, these black holes, to the Shining Star and the power of the cross, is going to do something and start the process in your life that can see nation's shaping. That can see your bloodline and your family totally whole.

For if, while we were God's enemies, we were reconciled to him through the death of his Son, how much more, having been reconciled, shall we be saved through his life! (Romans 5:10)

My father was a miner, a very gentle man, and a Catholic. He loved songs, and he used to sing a hymn to me as a little boy:

On a hill far away stood an old rugged cross,
The emblem of suffering and shame;
And I love that old cross where the dearest and best
For a world of lost sinners was slain.

So I'll cherish the old rugged cross,
Till my trophies at last I lay down;
I will cling to the old rugged cross,
And exchange it some day for a crown.

Here's a phenomenal story. I did a book signing in Sheffield and an unusual amount of people came from a church in Wickham, Manchester. So I'm saying, 'Hello, I'm Terry, where are you from?' to lots of people and then someone says to me, 'Oh but you'll want to meet Harry.' Harry comes through and says, 'Nice to meet you. Where are you from? I'm from Leigh.'

'Oh, I'm from Leigh,' I said. 'I'm from Higher Folds. Where d'you live in Leigh?'

He said, 'I live in Higher Folds!'

'Where d'you live? I lived on Royal Drive.'

He said, 'I live in the old Roman Catholic parsonage.'

Listen to this: my dad died when I was 13. Just after retiring he'd been working in the garden of this same Roman Catholic parsonage when he was found dead; they thought he was sunbathing. This same house. Isn't that an amazing story?

Our 'black hole' lives can be transformed so that we're shining stars through the power of the cross.

In that old rugged cross, stained with blood so divine,
A wondrous beauty I see,
For 'twas on that old cross Jesus suffered and died,
To pardon and sanctify me.

To pardon me. Not guilty. Acquitted in heaven's courts. Some of us are feeling guilty before a Holy God because of some of this stuff I've identified. So was I. Jesus, who was not sin, became sin that we might become the righteousness of God. What does righteous mean? Declared righteous, not guilty, acquitted in heaven's courts. Totally free. Pardoned and sanctified by the power and the regeneration of the Holy Spirit of God. God comes to live on the inside of us. And when you let God in, especially for those black holes, he fills you, and he sanctifies you, and you're regenerated. Our lives go from gory to glory.

There's a 'gory' every now and again. You go along in life and it's all glory. Then boom! You suddenly get a black hole. But let me encourage you: in my life, every 'gory' I hit, when I've allowed the black hole to become a shining star, it's just before the next level of glory. We go from glory to glory to glory. As we behold him, we're transformed and our lives are changed from one level of glory to the next.

We're pardoned, sanctified, regenerated by the power of the Holy Spirit. As we close this chapter the choice is yours: either hold on to the gaping black holes or small black holes, or you can allow God in his power to turn them into a shining star. The Lord sets you free totally. For some the release will be immediate; for others he'll start work on the inside of you, and it will grow and grow until that thing that was black and ugly and crippling you will be filled with his glory. You'll be totally free, redeemed, restored, a shining star.

Commendations

'Terry Eckersley is a remarkable man who has achieved an extraordinary amount. Yet as he admits, all that he has done is because of a God who, through his astonishing grace, rescued him from life's depths and changed him completely. The fact that God can transform a man like Terry today greatly encourages me in sharing the gospel. May Terry's story similarly inspire you!'

Revd Canon J.John, Philo Trust
www.canonjjohn.com

'Terry Eckersley is a gift to people who have faith and those far from it. Effervescent, engaging and never ceasing in seeking to be an encouragement, both as a public speaker and in the everyday conversations and contacts of life, Terry carries something that impacts and influences for good.'

Phil Pye, Arena Church – Ilkeston & Mansfield,
Member of National Leadership Team of AOG
www.arenachurch.co.uk

Meeting Terry Eckersley for the first time is a bit like opening a can of cola after it's been shaken up and down for a few minutes!

To say Terry can come across as a bubbling, effervescent extrovert would be about right, but there's more to him than meets the eye. He's a deep-thinking and thoughtful man who knows his God, knows God loves people, and knows his calling is to reach them on God's behalf.

I read and enjoyed the first half of this book whilst on a plane journey – and listening to my wife witnessing to the woman on the seat next to her. It was a practical demonstration of what Terry was explaining in writing

Part two of this book details the calling and practicalities of doing the *work of an evangelist – which you'll find informative and beneficial. It's good to be coached by people who are further along the road than you on these things – so read it with an open mind and heart – and then get out there and put it into practice!*

Bill Partington, Head of Affiliate Development, UCB Global Missions
www.ucb.co.uk

CHAPTER ONE

WHAT IS AN EVANGELIST?

Oxford Dictionary

1. A person who *seeks* to *convert others* to the Christian *faith*, especially by public *preaching*
2. A *layperson* engaged in Christian *missionary* work
3. A *zealous* advocate of a *particular cause*
4. The *writer* of one of the four *Gospels* (Matthew, Mark, Luke or John)

Do you fall into any of these categories? (Obviously not number 4!)

The term 'evangelist' is mentioned three times in the New Testament.

> *Leaving the next day, we reached Caesarea and stayed at the house of Philip the evangelist, one of the Seven.* (Acts 21:8)

This was Philip who proclaimed the gospel in Samaria and who also proclaimed the gospel to the Ethiopian eunuch in Acts 8.

> *So Christ himself gave the apostles, the prophets, the evangelists, the pastors and teachers, to equip his people for works of service, so that the body of Christ may be built up until we all reach unity in the faith and in the knowledge of the Son of God and become mature, attaining to the whole measure of the fullness of Christ.* (Ephesians 4:11–13)

Here the evangelist is presented as an office within the church. Interestingly, in terms of hierarchy the evangelist sits above pastors and teachers. The apostle plants the church, the prophet directs the church, the evangelist gathers the people, the pastor cares for the people and the teacher teaches the people.

> *But you, keep your head in all situations, endure hardship, do the work of an evangelist, discharge all the duties of your ministry.* (2 Timothy 4:5)

This was St Paul's charge to Timothy, to do evangelistic work. So we can see here that although someone may not have the office of the evangelist, they do still produce evangelistic activity. There are others in the New Testament who did the work of an evangelist – the most famous being St Peter and St Paul – but they were not described as evangelists; in fact they were apostles.

CHAPTER THREE

BIBLICAL EVANGELISTS

PHILIP

- scriptural knowledge
- authority through signs and wonders (anointing)
- baptism
- receiving the Holy Spirit
- personhood (married, Christian daughters)
- under the direction of the Spirit
- meeting a seeker where they are at

Those who had been scattered preached the word wherever they went. Philip went down to a city in Samaria and proclaimed the Messiah there. **When the crowds heard Philip and saw the signs he performed, they all paid close attention to what he said. For with shrieks, impure spirits came out of many, and many who were paralysed or lame were healed. So there was great joy in that city.**

Now for some time a man named Simon had practised sorcery in the city and amazed all the people of Samaria. He boasted that he was someone great, and all the people, both high and low, gave him their attention and exclaimed, 'This man is rightly called the Great Power of God.' They followed him because he had amazed them for a long time with his sorcery. **But when they believed Philip as he proclaimed the good news of the kingdom of God and the name of Jesus Christ, they were baptised, both men and women. Simon himself believed and was baptised. And he followed Philip everywhere, astonished by the great signs and miracles he saw.**

When the apostles in Jerusalem heard that Samaria had accepted the word of God, they sent Peter and John to Samaria. **When they arrived, they prayed for the new believers there that they might receive the Holy Spirit, because the Holy Spirit had not yet come on any of them; they had simply been baptised in the name of the Lord Jesus. Then Peter and John placed their hands on them, and they received the Holy Spirit.** (Acts 8:4–17; 26–40)

Now an angel of the Lord said to Philip, 'Go south to the road – the desert road – that goes down from Jerusalem to Gaza.' So he started out, *and on his way he met an Ethiopian eunuch, an important official in charge of all the treasury of the Kandake (which means 'queen of the Ethiopians'). This man had gone to Jerusalem to worship, and on his way home was sitting in his chariot reading the Book of Isaiah the prophet. The Spirit told Philip, 'Go to that chariot and stay near it.'*

Then Philip ran up to the chariot and heard the man reading Isaiah the prophet. **Do you understand what you are reading?'** *Philip asked.*

'How can I,' he said, 'unless someone explains it to me?' So he invited Philip to come up and sit with him.

This is the passage of Scripture the eunuch was reading:

'He was led like a sheep to the slaughter, and as a lamb before its shearer is silent, so he did not open his mouth. In his humiliation he was deprived of justice. Who can speak of his descendants? For his life was taken from the earth.' The eunuch asked Philip, 'Tell me, please, who is the prophet talking about, himself or someone else?' **Then Philip began with that very passage of Scripture and told him the good news about Jesus.**

As they travelled along the road, they came to some water and the eunuch said, 'Look, here is water. What can stand in the way of my being baptised?' And he gave orders to stop the chariot. **Then both Philip and the eunuch went down into the water and Philip baptised him.** *When they came up out of the water, the Spirit of the Lord suddenly took Philip away, and the eunuch did not see him again, but went on his way rejoicing. Philip, however, appeared at Azotus and travelled about, preaching the gospel in all the towns until he reached Caesarea.*

We continued our voyage from Tyre and landed at Ptolemais, where we greeted the brothers and sisters and stayed with them for a day. Leaving the next day, we reached Caesarea and stayed at the house of **Philip the evangelist, one of the Seven.** *He had four unmarried daughters who prophesied.* (Acts 21:7–9)

While Philip is given the official title of 'the evangelist, one of the Seven', there are many other examples of people in the Bible still performing evangelical acts without being given a specific title.

PETER

- Explanation of signs and wonders
- Pentecost – Peter addressed what they were saying

'Therefore let all Israel be assured of this: God has made this Jesus, whom you crucified, both Lord and Messiah.' When the people heard this, they were cut to the heart and said to Peter and the other apostles, 'Brothers, what shall we do?'

Peter replied, **Repent and be baptised, every one of you, in the name of Jesus Christ for the forgiveness of your sins. And you will receive the gift of the Holy Spirit. The promise is for you and your children and for all who are far off – for all whom the Lord our God will call.'**

With many other words he warned them; and he pleaded with them, 'Save yourselves from this corrupt generation.' Those who accepted his message were baptised, and about three thousand were added to their number that day. (Acts 2:36–41)

Calling people to Christ through repentance is therefore the key message of the evangelist, followed by calling and mobilising others to do the same. Keeping this message central is essential.

- Healing and use of this sign/wonder to preach the gospel

  While the man held on to Peter and John, all the people were astonished and came running to them in the place called Solomon's Colonnade. When Peter saw this, he said to them: 'Fellow Israelites, why does this surprise you? Why do you stare at us as if by our own power or godliness we had made this man walk? The God of Abraham, Isaac and Jacob, the God of our fathers, has glorified his servant Jesus. You handed him over to be killed, and you disowned him before Pilate, though he had decided to let him go. You disowned the Holy and Righteous One and asked that a murderer be released to you. You killed the author of life, but God raised him from the dead. We are witnesses of this. By faith in the name of Jesus, this man whom you see and know was made strong. It is Jesus' name and the faith that comes through him that has completely healed him, as you can all see. (Acts 3:11–20)

  'Now, fellow Israelites, I know that you acted in ignorance, as did your leaders. But this is how God fulfilled what he had foretold through all the prophets, saying that his Messiah would suffer. **Repent, then, and turn to God, so that your sins may be wiped out, that times of refreshing may come from the Lord, and that he may send the Messiah, who has been appointed for you – even Jesus.**

Healing is part of the call of the ascension gift of evangelism; praying for the sick is a command. Apostolic power is evident in the evangelist and as we see here, the 'dinner bell' for the gospel.

- Salvation whilst Peter is preaching (anointing)

  'We are witnesses of everything he did in the country of the Jews and in Jerusalem. They killed him by hanging him on a cross,

but God raised him from the dead on the third day and caused him to be seen. He was not seen by all the people, but by witnesses whom God had already chosen – by us who ate and drank with him after he rose from the dead. He commanded us to preach to the people and to testify that he is the one whom God appointed as judge of the living and the dead. All the prophets testify about him that everyone who believes in him receives forgiveness of sins through his name.'

While Peter was still speaking these words, the Holy Spirit came on all who heard the message. The circumcised believers who had come with Peter were astonished that the gift of the Holy Spirit had been poured out even on Gentiles. For they heard them speaking in tongues and praising God. *Then Peter said, 'Surely no one can stand in the way of their being baptised with water. They have received the Holy Spirit just as we have.* (Acts 10:39–47)

PAUL

* The book of Acts tells of all of the preaching tours that Paul undertook. Here we will just look at what Paul said about his calling to preach the gospel.

I myself am convinced, my brothers and sisters, that you yourselves are full of goodness, filled with knowledge and competent to instruct one another. Yet I have written you quite boldly on some points to remind you of them again, because of the grace God gave me to be a minister of Christ Jesus to the Gentiles. ***He gave me the priestly duty of proclaiming the gospel of God, so that the Gentiles*** *might become an offering acceptable to God, sanctified by the Holy Spirit.*

*Therefore I glory in Christ Jesus in my service to God. I will not venture to speak of anything except what Christ has accomplished through me in leading the Gentiles to obey God by what I have said and done – **by the power of signs and wonders, through the power of the Spirit of God.*** *So from Jerusalem* *all the way around to Illyricum, **I have fully proclaimed the gospel of Christ. It has always been my ambition to preach the gospel where Christ was not known,** so that I would not be building on someone else's foundation. Rather, as it is written: 'Those who were not told about him will see, and those who have not heard will understand.'* (Romans 15:14–21)

Paul preached without pretence, without pride. He preached only the gospel, and was not focused on his own ability to deliver it. God uses us where, and as, we are. All wisdom comes not from us, but from God speaking through us, and the Holy Spirit translating the message into the hearts of those who have ears to hear. Our efforts – our words, our delivery – do not bring salvation: only the Living Word of God which speaks to hearts brings salvation.

For Christ did not send me to baptise, but to preach the gospel – not with wisdom and eloquence, lest the cross of Christ be emptied of its power. (1 Corinthians 1:17)

Now when I went to Troas to preach the gospel of Christ and found that the Lord had opened a door for me. (2 Corinthians 2:12)

BARNABAS

- graced for taking the gospel to the Gentiles
- laying on of hands
- led by the Holy Spirit
- authority to confirm and encourage the work others had been doing
- personhood

    Now those who had been scattered by the persecution that broke out when Stephen was killed travelled as far as Phoenicia, Cyprus and Antioch, spreading the word only among Jews. Some of them, however, men from Cyprus and Cyrene, went to Antioch and began to speak to Greeks also, telling them the good news about the Lord Jesus. The Lord's hand was with them, and a great number of people believed and turned to the Lord. News of this reached the church in Jerusalem, and they sent Barnabas to Antioch. When he arrived and saw what the grace of God had done, he was glad and encouraged them all to remain true to the Lord with all their hearts. He was a good man, full of the Holy Spirit and faith, and a great number of people were brought to the Lord. (Acts 11:19–24)

While they were worshipping the Lord and fasting, the Holy Spirit said, 'Set apart for me Barnabas and Saul for the work to which I have called them.' So after they had fasted and prayed, they placed their hands on them and sent them off. The two of them, sent on their way by the Holy Spirit, went down to Seleucia and sailed from there to Cyprus. When they arrived at Salamis, they proclaimed the word of God in the Jewish synagogues. (Acts 13:2–5)

Then Paul and Barnabas answered them boldly: 'We had to speak the word of God to you first. Since you reject it and do not consider yourselves worthy of eternal life, we now turn to the Gentiles.' (Acts 13:46)

At Iconium Paul and Barnabas went as usual into the Jewish synagogue. There they spoke so effectively that a great number of Jews and Greeks believed. But the Jews who refused to believe stirred up the other Gentiles and poisoned their minds against the brothers. So Paul and Barnabas spent considerable time there, speaking boldly for the Lord, who confirmed the message of his grace by enabling them to perform signs and wonders. (Acts 14:1–3)

TIMOTHY

- encourager
- perseverance
- prepared for any type of reception of the word

  We sent Timothy, who is our brother and co-worker in God's service in spreading the gospel of Christ, to strengthen and encourage you in your faith. (1 Thessalonians 3:2)

For the Son of God, Jesus Christ, who was preached among you by us – by me and Silas and Timothy – was not 'Yes' and 'No', but in him it has always been 'Yes'. (2 Corinthians 1:19)

But you, keep your head in all situations, endure hardship, do the work of an evangelist, discharge all the duties of your ministry. (2 Timothy 4:5)

ALL OTHER BELIEVERS

- unity in the Spirit – the Spirit responds to a group of united believers
- persecution often has a counter-effect: the word is spread further and to more people despite intense opposition
- boldness in bringing the message

On their release, Peter and John went back to their own people and reported all that the chief priests and the elders had said to them. When they heard this, they raised their voices together in prayer to God. 'Sovereign Lord,' they said, 'you made the heavens and the earth and the sea, and everything in them. You spoke by the Holy Spirit through the mouth of your servant, our father David: "Why do the nations rage and the peoples plot in vain? The kings of the earth rise up and the rulers band together against the Lord and against his anointed one." Indeed Herod and Pontius Pilate met together with the Gentiles and the people of Israel in this city to conspire against your holy servant Jesus, whom you anointed. They did what your power and will had decided beforehand should happen. Now, Lord, consider their threats and enable your servants to speak your word with great boldness. Stretch out your hand to heal and perform signs and wonders through the name of your holy servant Jesus.' (Acts 4:23–31)

After they prayed, the place where they were meeting was shaken. ***And they were all filled with the Holy Spirit and spoke the word of God boldly.***

Now those who had been scattered by the persecution that broke out when Stephen was killed travelled as far as Phoenicia, Cyprus and Antioch, spreading the word only among Jews. Some of them, however, men from Cyprus and Cyrene, went to Antioch and began to speak to Greeks also, telling them the good news about the Lord Jesus. The Lord's hand was with them, and a great number of people believed and turned to the Lord. (Acts 11:19–21)

'Do not get any gold or silver or copper to take with you in your belts – no bag for the journey or extra shirt or sandals or a staff, for the worker is worth his keep.' (Matthew 10:9–10)

Next we will look at ways for an evangelist to make a living.

Self-support: tent-making and other employment

After this, Paul left Athens and went to Corinth. There he met a Jew named Aquila, a native of Pontus, who had recently come from Italy with his wife Priscilla, because Claudius had ordered all Jews to leave Rome. Paul went to see them, and because he was a tentmaker as they were, he stayed and worked with them. Every Sabbath he reasoned in the synagogue, trying to persuade Jews and Greeks. (Acts 18:1–4)

From this passage we can see that Paul worked as a tentmaker during the week and preached the gospel of a Saturday.

For further reading on why Paul worked a day job, see the following: http://www.bible-bridge.com/pauls-income-four-reasons-why-paul-worked-day-job/

RESEARCH ACTIVITY

Expound various ways and means, with examples.

Gifts and offerings

- Do you stipulate an amount you require or do you just trust God to give you whatever you need?

- Do you take up love offerings for your ministry?

The elderly elder [of the church addresses this letter] to the beloved (esteemed) Gaius, whom I truly love. Beloved, I pray that you may prosper in every way and [that your body] may keep well, even as [I know] your soul keeps well and prospers. In fact, I greatly rejoiced when [some of] the brethren from time to time arrived and spoke [so highly] of the sincerity and fidelity of your life, as indeed you do live in the Truth [the whole Gospel presents]. I have no greater joy than this, to hear that my [spiritual] children are living their lives in the Truth. Beloved, it is a fine and faithful work that you are doing when you give any service to the [Christian] brethren, and [especially when they are] strangers. They have testified before the church of your love and friendship. You will do well to forward them on their journey [and you will please do so] in a way worthy of God's [service]. For these [travelling missionaries] have gone out for the Name's sake (for His sake) and are accepting nothing from the Gentiles (the heathen, the non-Israelites). So we ourselves ought to support such people [to welcome and provide for them], in order that we may be fellow workers in the Truth (the whole Gospel) and cooperate with its teachers. (3 John 1–8 AMP)

Monthly support from churches

- When you work as an evangelist for a number of churches on a regular basis, you can set up an agreed remuneration

Trust/charity

- Establish a trust/charity to raise funds
  Example: Billy Graham Evangelistic Association

Christian Stewardship

- Online giving portal

Resources

- Sell books, DVDs, downloads, subscriptions to podcasts

CHAPTER SIX

PERSONHOOD

We can all get caught up with 'titles' and 'positions' but remember: we are all fallible human beings at the end of the day. Evangelists have the same life challenges as everyone else and they are normal like everyone else; this means they, too, mess up. When asked who you are the answer should not be 'I am an evangelist'; it should be 'I am a son, daughter, father, mother,' etc. A job title does not define who a person is. We define the 'Who are you?' as Personhood.

Personhood is incredibly important, not just in the life of an evangelist but in the life of every Christian. The gift and calling of God can get you there but good character keeps you there! As previously stated we know that we all mess up from time to time, but as you can see in the media, people of prominent position get lambasted very quickly if they make a character mistake. We do have an enemy: the accuser of the brethren will jump on any mistake. God's grace is never ending, but people are different.

Personhood, however, is not just about self-discipline and guarding oneself against the enemy. It's all about life balance. Granted, Jesus did not promise an easy life, but you can enjoy the journey. After all, he came to give us life, and abundant life, and to turn our grief into joy!

So how do we get into 'good shape'?

Personhood more or less consists of the following elements:

1. Spiritual Life

2. Health

3. Family Life

4. Work Life

5. Finances

6. Friends / Social Life / Spare Time

These are the areas of life that can make or break us.

In fact, all of our needs and barriers to our calling are interwoven in the above.

Growing things change, and changing things grow. The key to progression is CHANGE. You cannot expect a different outcome by doing the same thing over and over. Perform the following self-audit giving yourself a score of between 1 (weak) to 10 (strong). You may find much that needs changing, but the key to ongoing success is honesty with yourself, and setting yourself small, achievable goals. All these smaller changes add up to a BIG change.

Small goals are achievable.

Achieving goals boosts your confidence.

Confidence keeps the momentum going!

Examples could be: reading your Bible every day, doing exercise for four hours a week, reconfiguring your household budget in order to save 10 per cent a week . . .

SELF AUDIT

Area
Score (1-10)
Goal (What? By when?)
! Remember: ? small ? achievable
Spiritual Life
Health
Family Life
Work Life
Finances
Friends/Social Life/Spare Time

'The Modesto Manifesto'

Billy Graham and his team resolved:

1. To never exaggerate attendance figures at their meetings.
    Guard against lying and deceit.

2. To take only a fixed salary from their organisation. Guard against financial thievery.

3. To never be alone with a woman other than their wife, mother, daughters. Guard against sexual sin. (Even guard against any potential appearance of it!)

4. To never criticise fellow members of the clergy. Guard against pride.

The 100 per cent non-negotiable requirement: holiness!

> *Make every effort to live in peace with all men and be holy; without holiness no one will see the Lord.* (Hebrews 12:14)

What does 'being holy' mean?

Holiness is a description of God.

> *Each of the four living creatures had six wings and was covered with eyes all around, even under its wings. Day and night they never stop saying: 'Holy, holy, holy is the Lord God Almighty, who was, and is, and is to come.'* (Revelation 4:8)

So we can say that being holy is being God-like.

How are we to be holy? How can we be like God when we are mere humans?

We have the perfect example: Jesus the God-man!

All we have to do is copy Jesus.

> *We know that we have come to know him if we keep his commands. Whoever says, 'I know him,' but does not do what he commands is a liar, and the truth is not in that person. But if anyone obeys his word, love for God is truly made complete in them. This is how we know we are in him: Whoever claims to live in him must live as Jesus did.* (1 John 2:3–6)

A note on sin:

Holiness is synonymous with purity and sinlessness. God does not sin. But we do. How does that work then?

Well, it's purely a matter of decision making. Make the right decisions! There are three types of sin:

1. Original sin: performed in the Garden of Eden by Adam and Eve. This sin is in all of us and there is nothing we can do about it. This is totally covered by the blood of Christ.

2. Wilful sin: wilfully going against God's commands. Doing something wrong when you know it's wrong. This requires confession and repentance. When Jesus dealt with the woman at the well he told her to go 'and sin no more'. He did not say go 'and sin less'. The only unforgivable sin, the sin of unbelief and refusing to accept the sacrifice and salvation of the Son of God, falls into this category.

3. Sin of ignorance: sinning when you do not know it is a sin. When this happens one usually has an uncomfortable feeling about what has happened. Conviction of the Holy Spirit. If this happens then confess it to the Lord and move on.

So, the only sin you have control over is wilful sin.

We are declared positionally righteous and holy by the blood of Jesus alone. We can, however, through repentance and the power of Almighty God working within us, walk in purity, the fruit of the Holy Spirit. Jesus is Lord and Saviour, Author and Finisher of our faith.

Humility

Oxford Dictionary: The quality of having a low estimate of one's own importance.

> *Now Moses was a very humble man, more humble than anyone else on the face of the earth.* (Numbers 12:3)

> *Take my yoke upon you and learn from me, for I am gentle and humble in heart, and you will find rest for your souls. For my yoke is easy and my burden is light.* (Matthew 11:29–30)

For most people, 'being humble' brings to mind a form of weakness. 'If someone practises humility, it means they're not a "go-getter" and don't care about performance or working hard. It's the weak one who is humble and is dependent on someone else.' If this is true, why do you suppose the Bible has so much to say about being humble? Maybe we've got it all wrong and the one who practises humility is actually the strong one?

Humble yourselves, therefore, under God's mighty hand, that he may lift you up in due time. Cast all your anxiety on him because he cares for you. (1 Peter 5:6–7)

God cares for us. He is mighty. He calls us to humble ourselves under him. Not because he is a controlling God that wants you to bow down to him because you are nothing, but rather because he wants to exalt us and care for us. As we humble ourselves, that is when we truly worship him in Spirit and in truth; when we're trusting him with what's going on in our lives and believing he is the provider instead of ourselves.

Stop putting everything on your shoulders

Are you busy? Are you weary? Are you taking on a lot of responsibilities? Are you working hard for your family? Are you trying to attend as many social events as possible? Are you trying to pay the bills as best as you can? Are you striving, just to 'get by'?

'Come to me, all you who are weary and burdened, and I will give you rest. Take my yoke upon you and learn from me, for I am gentle and humble in heart, and you will find rest for your souls. For my yoke is easy and my burden is light.' (Matthew 11:28–30)

Jesus doesn't seem to be describing a life full of anxiety and weariness in following him. He makes a point to state the exact opposite of how we can find rest in him! He is speaking to those that labour and are heavy laden.

Are we working too hard? Are we thinking way too much? Are we putting things on our shoulders that don't belong there? Are we forgetting what Jesus said and what he has done when we feel that it's 'all on us' to get things to happen? Most of the time, we're probably putting so much effort into all the wrong things.

In today's culture, we're told if you labour and are heavy laden then you are doing the right thing. You are sacrificing for your family and friends. You are pulling yourself up by your bootstraps and working hard to hopefully one day achieve paradise (retirement) where you get to do nothing as you live out the rest of your days. This is wrong. Don't let culture tell you that putting everything on your shoulders is wisdom. Trust Jesus when he tells you that his burden is light.

> *Rejoice in the Lord always. I will say it again: rejoice! Let your gentleness be evident to all. The Lord is near. Do not be anxious about anything, but in every situation, by prayer and petition, with thanksgiving, present your requests to God. And the peace of God, which transcends all understanding, will guard your hearts and your minds in Christ Jesus. Finally, brothers and sisters, whatever is true, whatever is noble, whatever is right, whatever is pure, whatever is lovely, whatever is admirable – if anything is excellent or praiseworthy – think about such things. Whatever you have learned or received or heard from me, or seen in me – put it into practice. And the God of peace will be with you.* (Philippians 4:4–9)

When we don't humble ourselves, we are really saying that we don't trust God. There are times as a follower of Christ when we forget God's character or doubt him. We're told in Scripture to think on the things of God, to meditate on anything worthy of praise.

These things that are true, honourable, just, pure, lovely, commendable, or excellent are all praiseworthy because God is all these things. You'll never find an area of the Bible that contradicts God's character, and that should encourage us in those moments of doubt.

God gave his one and only son for us. This tells us a lot about his character. That doesn't sound like a God who is a tyrant and just demands power all the time. It doesn't match up to a God that doesn't care about us. He knew that we could only come to him through his son who had to suffer and die before rising again. With that perfect knowledge, which only God can have, he followed through and sacrificed his son for us. Not only does that tell us everything we need to know about God's character, that shows us just how much he loves us.

Jesus is our ultimate example of humility. Out of obedience to his Father, he humbled himself all the way to the point of death on the cross.

> *And being found in appearance as a man, he humbled himself by becoming obedient to death – even death on a cross!* (Philippians 2:8–11)

Therefore God exalted him to the highest place and gave him the name that is above every name, that at the name of Jesus every knee should bow, in heaven and on earth and under the earth, and every tongue acknowledge that Jesus Christ is Lord, to the glory of God the Father.

If Jesus practised humility himself, then why would we think we don't need to? Why would we consider this to be weakness? Even he was dependent on his Father and this was a good thing; in fact, the best thing. It was a God glorifying thing in every way. We couldn't even have a relationship with God if it wasn't for what Jesus did for us in the first place. We had to humble ourselves to trust that Jesus is King and to ask him to be our Lord and Saviour. This is no different today whether you've been a believer for a week or 50 years.

We still need him in everything we do. We still need the Holy Spirit to guide us and give us wisdom in all matters. We still need help to practise things that are honourable, pure, lovely, commendable, or anything praiseworthy. We are still not capable of doing anything on our own and will never be. As soon as we begin to live in a way where we are no longer dependent on God to do everything for us, we are forgetting our first love and proclaiming what Christ did for us was not enough.

As a follower of Christ, no matter what circumstance you find yourself in, you can give it to him. This is because God's Word is true. What Jesus did was enough. And you have the Holy Spirit and can trust him to lead and guide you. Humble yourself and pray to God, truly casting your anxieties on Him and trust that he does indeed care for you.

CHAPTER SEVEN

SHARING THE MESSAGE

The message of the evangelist in simple: KISS! (Keep It Simple, Sanctified!) God loves you: Jesus died for you. Turn from your sin (missing the mark), and turn to the finished work of Jesus on the cross for forgiveness of your sins. Bringing people to assurance of Salvation is imperative and here's where reliance on the work and person of the Holy Spirit is also essential.

> *For God so loved the world that he gave his one and only Son, that whoever believes in him shall not perish but have eternal life.* (John 3:16)

> *And I will ask the Father, and he will give you another advocate to help you and be with you forever.* (John 14:16)

> *But you will receive power when the Holy Spirit comes on you; and you will be my witnesses in Jerusalem, and in all Judea and Samaria, and to the ends of the earth.* (Acts 1:8)

Etiquette and Ethical Protocol

*   Lines of communication
*   Relationships
*   Dos and don'ts

> *So Christ himself gave the apostles, the prophets, the evangelists, the pastors and teachers, to equip his people for works of service, so that the body of Christ may be built up until we all reach unity in the faith and in the knowledge of the Son of God and become mature, attaining to the whole measure of the fullness of Christ.* (Ephesians 4:11–13)

Build and keep a good relationship with those with other ascension gift ministries, as mentioned above. This is essential! Also, be careful when building relationships with congregation members, to respect the authority and role of the pastors and their teams: this will help prevent things getting messy.

Don't play on slippery slopes, that's how better people than you and I have fallen! As with the Billy Graham Modesto Manifesto, no time alone with anyone of the opposite sex outside of family.

What is the message?

- The gospel!
- What is the gospel? The good news of salvation through Jesus Christ!
- What is the call to salvation? It is surrendering your life to Christ: Giving your will for your life over to God's will.

Therefore, I urge you, brothers and sisters, in view of God's mercy, to offer your bodies as a living sacrifice, holy and pleasing to God – this is your true and proper worship. Do not conform to the pattern of this world, but be transformed by the renewing of your mind. Then you will be able to test and approve what God's will is – his good, pleasing and perfect will. (Romans 12:1–2)

We must share a message of complete surrender at the first opportunity, surrendering our lives to God's salvation plan for our lives. This is good news! God's redemptive plan is a lot better than any we have.

How to convey the message

The Art of Storytelling

The gift of the evangelist often carries the art of storytelling. Many of the greats – D.L. Moody, George Whitfield, and our modern-day friend J.John – use storytelling to give powerful illustrations and anecdotes. Why not study and sharpen these gifts and communication skills that allow us to engage with unbelievers in a powerful and relevant way, without losing the potency of the gospel, the Spirit and the Word of God.

Altar Calls

These can be many and varied. Reflect on the first 'altar call' given after Jesus' ascension:

> *When the people heard this, they were cut to the heart and said to Peter and the other apostles, 'Brothers, what shall we do?' Peter replied, 'Repent and be baptised, every one of you, in the name of Jesus Christ for the forgiveness of your sins. And you will receive the gift of the Holy Spirit. The promise is for you and your children and for all who are far off – for all whom the Lord our God will call.' With many other words he warned them; and he pleaded with them, 'Save yourselves from this corrupt generation.' Those who accepted his message were baptised, and about three thousand were added to their number that day.* (Acts 2:37–41)

As Peter in Acts 2:1–36 laid out the sinfulness of man, so, too, Jonathan Edwards (a great awakening revivalist) preached of sinners in the hands of an angry God! However, the wrath of God is then *fully satisfied* in the finished work of Jesus on the cross!

Inviting Jesus into your heart and life:

1. There is a heaven to gain! (Good news to rejoice in!)
2. There is a hell to shun. (Reality to be aware of.)
3. There is a need: to turn from our sin. (Meaning of sin = missing the mark.)
4. There is a decision to be made. (To follow Jesus, take up our cross daily, die to self, i.e. anything where my will is in conflict with God's will, Word, Spirit.)

Mobilising: equipping the saints/congregants into works of service

Ephesians 4:11–13 again!
Training the people, teaching the people (the people = the Church = the Body of Christ):

- Who they are in Christ.

- What they have in Christ (i.e. ALL we need for life and godliness).

And then, how to share the good news out of a spiritual overflow. (We ALL have an anointing and are commissioned to win the lost, not just the evangelist.)

The Hard Facts

Fact 1. Not many win people to Christ or even share their faith.
Fact 2. Not many want to or desire to.
Fact 3. Not many find it easy to build friendships with non-believers.

We *have to* address the above. How can we do this?

1. **Stay on fire ourselves and be practitioners.** D.L. Moody sought to win at least one person daily to Christ. Yes, this will take continued prayer, study and action! Keeping this at the forefront of our hearts, minds and actions. Be intentional about soul winning.

2. **Then we can authentically equip others** to do the same. The power is in the gospel, not us. We are the messengers.

Impartation

Impartation is being around bigger ministries than ourselves, the smearing, the mentorship from another. The laying on of hands, stirring up the gift that is in you.

> *For this reason I remind you to fan into flame the gift of God,*
> *which is in you through the laying on of my hands.*
> (2 Timothy 1:6)

The apostle Paul writes to his young protégé Timothy, encouraging him to do the work of an evangelist, to fan his gift into flame, to stay on fire!

Follow up/next steps discipleship

- Use resources: DVDs, CDs, online resources, booklets (both your own work and that of others)

- Lock into the local church, work with the local church

- Encourage participation in discipleship courses and developing a lifestyle that is accountable to and consistent with the Word of God

Raising Evangelists

Seek to mentor and help others with the same heart and call of the evangelist. Reach up and reach down. Help in lifting them up and getting them established. We are all on that journey, and we all need help along the way.

Barriers

What issues have you faced in the area of evangelism?

Lacking finance/provision?

We need to overcome this; each for their own ministry and to help others in their ministries.

1. Believe God: he is our source.

2. Tap into Christian stewardship, sowing and reaping, raising partners, major donors, targeted fundraising, multiple income streams, church support, gifts and offerings; knowing full well that where God guides, he provides; where he leads, he feeds! These are not just clichés but powerful, fundamental truths.

Lacking opportunities?

1. Pray.

2. Find a way to promote and market your ministry.

3. Network! Keep building relationships, and make use of the ones you already have!

4. Ask for recommendations.

5. Go! Even whilst we are praying and waiting for the above, the command is to go now! Start with what you have. We can tell ourselves and the devil, we will win souls one-on-one whilst we are waiting! And because you've gone after and valued the souls that nobody else wants, you'll get the souls that everybody wants! We have seen this.

Lacking credibility?

1. Stay planted in the local church.

2. Maintain good friendships.

3. Stay planted in your close and *affirming family*. (Be warned: not all will affirm the call of God on your life.)

4. Ask for references from credible ministries and friends.

5. Stay true to the Word of God. Live it!

6. Live a holy and humble life; be quick to repent and keep close accounts with God and friends.

Experiencing loneliness?

This goes with the territory. It can be very lonely at times. That's why it's important, and I emphasise again, stay in church, stay close to God and the comfort of the Holy Spirit. Time alone with God in study and prayer is essential.

Experiencing inconsistency?

Keep doing the right things, over and over and over again!

Needs

- Coaching/affirmation: get friendly and stay close to those who have gone before you.

- Anointing: stay under the anointing – the empowerment of God to do the task. Never put your trust or confidence in your own strength or ability.

- DSPs (divine strategic partnerships): Ask! God will give you these. In Luke 5, Peter needed friends to bring in the largest catch ever! So do we! Signal to friends in other boats – churches, ministries, callings, supporters. Again, reach up and down. Pray, look, knock and know that Jesus – who is the same yesterday, today and forever (Hebrews 13:8) – still provides.

CHAPTER EIGHT

ONE-ON-ONE EVANGELISM

Tips on where to start with one-on-one evangelism . . .

So, everybody's different right? No two people speak exactly the same way, look the same, smell the same, and dress the same. One thing that is common to many Christians I've met, however, is a difficulty when it comes to sharing their faith. I'm not sure it was meant to be that way. I've mentioned before that when we look at the early church in the book of Acts, they went out in the boldness and power of the Holy Spirit and not a lot of fear! For a lot of people today, fear seems to be the major issue – being afraid of what others may think or may say. Well here are five things that hopefully will be a starting point to help you overcome those fears if you struggle to share your faith . . .

1.   Pray

This is obviously not rocket science but as someone (John Wesley, I think?) said, 'Before we talk to the people about God, we need to talk to God about the people!' We can never be effective in our witnessing and evangelism if we don't pray.

2.   Rely on the Holy Spirit

German evangelist Reinhard Bonnke says, 'The Holy Spirit is the master evangelist.' A whole number of blogs could be written on this one subject, but the key thing for us to realise is that it is not down to us to save the world – Jesus is the Saviour and the Holy Spirit brings conversion (John 16:7–12). Our job is to share the gospel and we do that best when we rely on the Holy Spirit to prompt us, empower us and equip us with the words to say!

3. Share your story

So many people say 'I'm not called to be an evangelist'. Well maybe not, but we are all called to be witnesses (Acts 1:7–9). That means telling our story of how Jesus changed our lives. We may not feel we have the gifting or training of an evangelist (yet!) but we do have our own experience of knowing Jesus. Telling your story is a great place to start when it comes to evangelism!

4. Don't feel guilty

As I've mentioned, so many people feel guilty about the fact that they have not been sharing their faith. They want to do more, they try to do more, but it just doesn't seem to happen. The enemy is very good at making us feel guilty. One word of advice: relax. Yes, the gospel is urgent and we need to get on with the job of telling people, but sometimes we can run ahead of ourselves and we try to do things in our own strength instead of taking the time to pray and trust the Holy Spirit! Having said that, I've had times I've felt prompted by the Holy Spirit to say something to someone and have just shrugged it off. If we miss an opportunity we just have to repent and ask the Lord to open up another one, and try to be ready when that one comes along!

5. Don't be afraid to say 'I don't know'

Quite often we can be held back from witnessing because we feel inadequate. We don't feel we have enough knowledge. We're worried someone might ask us a difficult question and we won't know how to answer it. There are two ways to deal with this problem. The first is to have the courage to say 'I don't know' – but then we need to follow that with 'but I'll try to find out'. Maybe meet the person with your pastor or find someone else who will help you answer the question. (One thing we do need to try to discern is if the question is genuine or not.) The second way to help with this issue is for us to know the Bible as best we can, read it regularly and to commit to memory certain Bible verses that we feel will be helpful to us in our witnessing. It's amazing how the Holy Spirit can bring a verse back to our minds at just the right time!

Steve Mullins (Dry Bones Trust)

www.drybonestrust.org

Training and equipping the local church: 5 sessions over a weekend with a local church

1. It's Time to Flourish

2. It's All Working Out

3. Don't Deny the Power

4. Beyond the Open Door

5. Divine Strategic Partnership

The simplest tool you'll ever use . . .

The4points

One of the ways you can start a conversation with someone is to give them one of the hand-out cards. You'll see on this card a heart, a multiplication sign, a cross (as in the cross of Christ), then a question mark. There you go. So really, it's the gospel made simple. I say, can the simple gospel message really change people's lives today? Can it? Are you sure? Are you really sure? Absolutely!

A simple gospel message can still change people's lives today.

First point: God loves me.
Second point: I have sinned.
Third point: Jesus died for me.
Fourth point: I need to decide to live for God.

And then you can see the prayer at the end. I mean, how simple can that be?

For examples of one-on-one evangelism conversations and further explanation of the4points, please see Appendix 1.

CHAPTER NINE

THE CHURCH:
STAYING PLANTED IN THE FAMILY

The righteous will flourish like a palm tree, they will grow like a cedar of Lebanon; planted in the house of the LORD, they will flourish in the courts of our God. They will still bear fruit in old age, they will stay fresh and green. (Psalm 92:12–14)

Prerequisites always bring promises!

1. We will flourish.
2. We will bear fruit.
3. We will stay fresh.

Staying planted in your local church is absolutely essential and non-negotiable for personal health, scriptural obedience and credibility. This is one of the things (if not the main thing!) that has kept me – and many others – 'on the straight and narrow' over the years. A coal burns much brighter when with other coals. The church is God's family, where we are cared for, mobilised, loved, taught and enjoy fun, friendship and food. It's what Christ is committed to building and the gates of hell will not prevail against it! No church is perfect; if you find a 'perfect' one don't join that or you'll make it imperfect! (Joke!) When people are looking for the perfect church, they are always disappointed because it doesn't exist! Not yet, anyway.

Guidelines on staying planted:

1. Remember, your church is home.
2. Try to attend your home church at least once a month.
3. Build and maintain good relationships, especially with the leader(s).
4. Give.

5. Receive.

6. Be an active part of your church.

7. Speak well of your church, leaders, fellow worshippers. Be an encourager!

RECOMMENDED READING

Chasing the Dragon (Jackie Pullinger)
The Cross and the Switchblade (David Wilkerson)
Living a Life of Fire (Reinhard Bonnke)
Biographies of: George Whitefield, D.L. Moody, Hudson Taylor

APPENDIX 1:

TRANSCRIPT OF TRAINING SESSION – THE4POINTS

Welcome to the first Evangelist Academy that we're doing in this manner. I feel very honoured and very excited! This is very key, what we're doing today; it's so important, it's so the heart of God, it's so the will of God, so with us, for us, behind us, it's the heart of the Christian faith. We've got the great commandment: 'Love one another'; and then we've got the great commission: 'Go, seek the lost, make disciples of all nations' – for you are disciples! So we're going to share about a bit. We're going to demystify and take away some fear factors around one-on-one evangelism, because really, God doesn't tell us to do anything that isn't out of our league or zone. 'Oh well, I'm not an evangelist,' you say. Well, you might not be, but I am, and the gift of the evangelist is to train you and to mobilise you and to impart into you, *so you can do the work* of the evangelist. Paul said that to Timothy, didn't he? 2 Timothy 3:5 says, 'Having a form of godliness but denying its power. Have nothing to do with such people.' The answer to 2 Timothy 3:5 is actually 2 Timothy 4:5 – 'But you, keep your head in all situations, endure hardship, do the work of an evangelist, discharge all the duties of your ministry.' He says that to the pastors, and we know pastors have got the heart for evangelism!

So that's just a bit of an introduction. I'm going to read a couple of scriptures and then we'll do some training, some praying, and then we're going to go out in teams, and meet back here afterwards. Let's just pray before we start.

Lord Jesus, we thank you that your heart is to come and seek, and save that which was lost. Thank you that that's why you came, Lord, to seek and save those that are lost, to destroy the works of the enemy, and you came that we might have life, and have it more abundantly. Lord, we lift this Evangelist Academy session to you, we ask for your anointing on your word, Lord, and on this training. We pray for impartation and empowerment, and we pray for the labourers, Lord, that are here today, and for anointing as we go – for we know that the harvest is ripe, the fields are ripened to harvest! We pray that hearts will be open and receptive, Lord. As we go, we pray for your protection, we pray for your joy, your spirit of fun and adventure, Lord. Anoint everybody here, Lord, and anybody who listens to this within the sound of my voice, or from reading these words, with the anointing of evangelism, Lord, the gift of the evangelist released and stood up for you – that people may be one for you, in the name of Jesus. And everybody said? 'Amen.'

If you've got your Bibles with you, turn to Mark 16:15–17.

And then he told them, 'Go into all the world and preach the good news to everyone. Anyone who believes and is baptised will be saved, but anyone who refuses to believe will be condemned. These miraculous signs will accompany those who believe.'

Jesus is telling us to go and preach the gospel – the good news. Those who believe and receive will be saved; those who don't are damned already. That's a fact! Jill pulled a face then, questioning 'damned'. Well it's true, they are, like we were once damned, but we're not going to damn people, we're going to share the good news, and I'll talk more about that later. And the great thing about Jesus is, everything he asks us to do, he goes with us and he empowers us to do. Isn't that great? So we're really, really, fulfilling the great commission here today. We're fulfilling God's plan, and the prayer of Jesus, so all heaven is behind us, all heaven is literally on our side today. So be encouraged! There are people following us all around the UK and all around the world, and they're praying for us this morning. Isn't that great!

So, we're doing what Jesus wants us to do. Do you remember the wristbands? 'What would Jesus do?' Well, this is exactly what he would do, and did. You know what I mean? People used to make it all super-spiritual didn't they, 'What would Jesus do?' Jesus would do this, or do that. Well actually, he came to seek and save the lost, destroy the works of the enemy, and he came that we might have life and have it at its fullness. So that's good, isn't it? Amen forevermore!

Onto our next scripture, Luke 10:2 – and I'm only reading these two scriptures – why make it complicated?

'Then he said to them, "The harvest is plentiful, but the workers are few. Ask the Lord of the harvest, therefore, to send out workers into his harvest field."'

So we're fulfilling the prayer of Jesus, right here, right now, and the prayer of the early disciples. We, today, in this room, and those listening to the recording, or reading about it, are fulfilling the prayer of Jesus, fulfilling the great commission, and that really excites me. What is God's will for my life? This, this is it. If we can just keep this heart, and keep this spirit. . . I like John Wesley, who said this, 'God rewards those who go after souls.' He does. I've always been a soul winner, and God has always rewarded me. What scripture? Hebrews 11:6 says that we must first believe that God exists when we come to him, and secondly we must believe that he's a rewarder of those who diligently seek him. At no time can we see God more, than when we are diligently seeking him for the souls of men and women, boys and girls. Amen.

So, get ready for God openly rewarding you, and continuing to reward you as you continue to be a soul winner! Amen. Praise God! So I'm just going to share a little now about how we're going to do this soul winning. As I'm doing that, Jill is going to give everybody a free gift. Anybody like a free gift? Yes, of course – everyone likes a free gift! While that's happening, I'll just talk you through the soul-winning script which we're going to use today.

The4points

It's a four-point soul-winning script, and I really like these. I've spoken to Dave Sharples, who is the director of this Christian ministry. Since 1993 he's been a youth worker in Liverpool; he actually got an MBE! He worked with young people in Toxteth, which is like a ghetto, all the riots were in Toxteth – you might remember that. He tried to make the church more accessible and relevant to local families by communicating the gospel in a simple and memorable way. In 1995 he and his wife visited Metro Ministries in New York and were really inspired by the work of Bill Wilson – especially how he used a really simple way to communicate the essence of the gospel. It's called 'the four most important things in the world!' and is a mixture of the wordless gospel Spurgeon created way back in 1866 to explain the gospel to inner-city orphans in London, and the four spiritual laws tract written by Bill Bright in 1952. Anyway, Dave and the team started teaching the four most important things every week but changed the name to 'the4points' to make it simpler. Then in 2005 Dave and his friend Nick Gillard came up with this graphic logo based on the4points. They wanted to create a cryptic and intriguing mathematical equation that would spark conversations and help people to share their faith. They realised they had inadvertently created a tool for international evangelism that broke both the literacy and language barriers, which is amazing! They've got wristbands as well as the fold-out tracts, and the tracts can even be personalised on the back panel, to help with follow up, and are available in over twenty languages.

So look at the rich heritage we're tapping into here; it's great, isn't it? 'The Four Spiritual Laws' written by Bill Bright in 1952 and inspired by Spurgeon in the 1800s, then Bill Wilson with 'the four most important things', and now my friend Dave Sharples with the4points which I'm just going to talk you through now. In fact, we need to give everybody one of these; you can just take one and pass them round. It's the four points. Everybody say 'four points'. It's not a four-point sermon, it's just four points. It's not four points and a poem, it's just simply four points.

On the back it explains it more; I'll go through it. The4points is a very simple overview of the Bible. The first thing you need to know is that God is crazy about you, and it is unconditional. There is nothing you can do that will make God love you any more, or any less, than he already does right now. There is nothing God wants more than to love and be loved by humans. **First point.**

The second point: I have sinned. Sadly, we have been separated from God's love by something the Bible calls sin. Simply put, sin is when we do something to please ourselves rather than God. We sin when we ignore God, break his laws and basically do something our own way that is contrary to God's way. Sin destroys relationships with friends, with family and with God. The Bible says that sin, ultimately, brings death.

That's a great point, a really, really good point to share with people, and I'll explain more on this later.

So then, the wages of sin is death, but the gift of God is eternal life. We all want a free gift, don't we? Yes? We all want a free gift. You all wanted a free gift today, and that leads us to 'Jesus died for me'. **The third point** is probably one of the most well-known facts in the history of mankind, but is often misunderstood. The key is to realise that the penalty for sin is death. We've all sinned, and we all deserve to die, but God, who is full of mercy, loves you so much that he sent Jesus to die in your place. Jesus died so that we can have eternal life. It's a free gift.

Fourth point: I need to decide to live for God. Not only did Jesus die for our sin, but three days later he rose from the dead! Through his death and resurrection, Jesus now made a way for us to have a relationship with God. All you need to do is to accept that you've sinned, ask for God's forgiveness, and then decide to live the rest of your life for him. The choice is yours.

Then there's a prayer on the back. If you turn it over, you can see the four steps here, the four points: God loves me. I have sinned. Jesus died for me. I need to decide to live for God. And it looks really cool, doesn't it? Don't you think? I think it looks great; young people would like something like this. It looks like emoticon kind of speak, looks great, is really well produced. So this in itself would be a good gift, but we're going to do more than that because a lot of people just go and give tracks out and people don't really know why. But we're going to talk people through this and I'll explain to you how to do it and train you and help you to do it. But let's practise on one another before we go out.

And just while we're talking about this, what's really good about this method is it totally depersonalises it, i.e. it's really not dependent on you. You can point people to the script which is pointing people to the plan of redemption, the plan of salvation. I'll talk more about that, but it's really about keeping it simple, the KISS Principle: Keep It Simple Sanctified. Amen. So you've all been sanctified and we can keep it simple and I just want to give a couple of testimonies of how we have done this, Jill and I. You know, I could say I don't really need a script, because I don't; I do this all the time – my wife will tell you – everywhere I go I do it, I lead people to Christ. But for us all, now, this is a great tool for us all to use and not just today, but it will train you and equip you for the rest of your life. Just imagine this, right: we get to heaven and we're standing in front of Jesus and it's all going to be great, which it is, but there's a moment at the judgement seat of Christ, where we will all stand before Christ and be judged for everything we have done, or not done. Yes, we've been redeemed; yes, we've been forgiven. But we're going to be in the eternity of eternities and can you imagine getting to heaven and never actually leading anyone to Christ or bringing anyone with you or behind you? It's OK, you'll get in, but imagine the great rejoicing when people come to you and say, 'I'm so thankful that you shared the gospel with me. I'm so glad.' We're literally going to be snatching people from hell because there is a hell to shun and a heaven to gain. That's the good news that we're sharing.

So the first testimony that comes to mind was when we were in London. We were in five days of revival meetings at the O2 in London, just like we've been in here, meeting in here, getting touched by the power of God, getting refreshed, getting all this, but all that is so we can share the gospel. That's what it's all about; otherwise it's a total waste of time, a social club, a 'bless me' club. But we're blessed so we can go! So, Jill and I were at the O2 and we went out for lunch or a drink, and we were exploring around the O2 and we ended up in a VIP airport lounge, with stewardesses and stewards welcoming you. It was all very James Bond, very high tech and looked great, very cool, just opened. I love stuff like that. So we go in and they are showing us round and we're talking to the guy, who was very effeminate (I'm just setting the scene) and he's showing us this lounge and that lounge, and 'Would you like a drink?' So we sit down, are talking, he's telling us who he is and what he does and then he says to me, 'And what do you do?'

(Good question, isn't it? I said, 'Well, I'm glad you asked.' I said I'm like a modern-day missionary, that's what I am. That's a good way of putting it, isn't it? That's what you are, right now. And that's good, because it leads people to ask, 'What is a modern-day missionary?')

He wants to know more . . . 'Well, I go round the world and I tell people "God loves them, Jesus died for them and he's got a plan for their life."'

'Really, yeah, great, that's good. Well, actually, I used to go to church, been to church,' – don't get into the church thing with people; there's no need to do it, you'll just be there debating, arguing all day.

'Oh great, OK. Has anybody ever told you God loves you, Jesus died for you, and he's got a plan for your life?'

'Well, not really.'

'Well he does and he has. Did you know the wages of sin is death but the gift of God is eternal life?'

He does all the 'I'm a good guy, I've done good, I've done all this and that.'

'Oh, that's good. Did you know the Bible says all of us have fallen short of the glory of God?'

And it's like this: I've told him 'God loves me'. Now I'm moving onto 'I have sinned. You have sinned. Do you know you have sinned? We've all sinned, right, but Jesus died for you. The gift of God is eternal life, to all those who receive.' Now the next one: 'I need to decide to live for God.' So the gift of God is eternal life, and we all want a free gift, don't we? I've been saying that time and time again – it's a good point! So what do I do straight away then? I ask, 'Would you mind if I pray with you and for you?' Most times, nine times out of ten, people say, 'No I don't mind. Yes, please pray for me,' and this is what I do. You've got a script here, so you can actually read and pray the script over them. Or you can change it. *'Dear God, thank you that you love [Kevin / Steve / whatever their name is]. That you have a good plan and purpose for his life.'* And just pray blessing over them. That's what I did. *'Bless him, bless his family, give him a great life, empower him, pray good stuff and I pray that he'll accept you quickly. Amen.'*

'Would you like to accept Christ right now?' (It's what I said to him – would you like to? It's like closing the deal if you're in sales. Calling people to Christ. You've already prayed with him and for him, prayed good prayers.) 'Would you like to accept the free gift of salvation right now?'

'Yes.'

'Well OK, pray with me as I pray this prayer . . .

Dear Lord Jesus, come into my life, forgive me of my sin.' (Now all the stuff's on here you can pray.)

'Sorry for ignoring you and doing things my way. I realise now that my sin has hurt you and the people around me, and for this I'm truly sorry. Thank you, Jesus, that you gave your life for me and took the punishment for my sins. Please forgive me and help me now by the power of your Holy Spirit as I decide to live for you. Amen.'

Amen! Praise God! And then you can give them that. Now, I did that and the guy turned to me and said, 'Wow, can you feel that?!'

I said, 'Yes, I can feel that. I do feel that, I feel that all the time, everywhere I go.' I said, 'Not everyone feels it, but I'm so pleased you felt it.'

But he felt the anointing because we'd been saturated in meetings like you've been and something happens to you, and it'll never leave you. You receive an impartation and we'll pray that over you today before we go. But can you see how simple that is? Friends of ours take their children on the streets soul winning. Obviously they are with their parents and other trusted adults, but they go and all they are doing is using the script. This soul winning script. Amen!

Jill's going to tell you about another time we did that with somebody, led them to Christ.

[Jill] I probably had more input in the last example than this one. Actually the guy at the O2 was Catholic, so we asked him, 'If you were to die tonight, do you know where you would go?' He said, 'Oh, yes. I'd go to heaven because I'm a good boy and I've not done anything wrong.' And quite often people will say that: 'I'm a good person, I haven't done anything wrong.' I digress.

So, we were in Florida, in October and it was quite late, probably about one o'clock in the morning, and we were working our way back to our accommodation, when we stopped. We were trying to find somewhere to eat and we found this place called IHOP, International House of Pancakes (not International House of Prayer!), so in we went for something to eat and we were eating and chatting to the lady serving us. Very upbeat, very nice lady, and at the end this young lady had gone outside and we were getting ready to go and were heading towards the car and Terry thanks the young lady for serving us.

'Oh, why are you guys over here?'

'We're actually at a ministers' and leaders' conference.'

'Oh right,' and it turned out her sister was a Christian. Terry said, 'Do you know that God loves you and that Jesus died for you and has got a plan for your life?' I think at that point she just burst into tears, and said, 'Ahhh, you know, my sister is a Christian.' And I think she'd been going through quite a bad time, I think she'd been quite sick. Yes, she'd lost her husband, only a very young woman, maybe 30, and she was in absolutely streams of tears and Terry said, 'Well, God has obviously sent us here,' because nowhere else was open, everywhere else had just closed, just this one restaurant was open. 'God sent us to this place, by divine appointment so that we can pray with you.' And she accepted Christ and we actually saw her on another evening that week as well, and she was completely different. Although she was upbeat both times, you could see her face was different this time. You know, she didn't have that heaviness, didn't have that weight upon her.

Again, I think Terry probably just took her hand. I was there as well, so probably not a good idea for women to grab guy's hands or vice versa if they are not with other people – you know, make sure there is somebody with you. Just to be careful – you never know. Anyway, Terry prayed in Jesus's name and again she felt the presence of the Holy Spirit. I think often in church we don't realise how amazing this is, because we become familiar and we become used to the presence of God. Like the guy at the O2, he was like 'Can you feel that? Can you feel that?!' because he had never before felt the presence of God. So often we can think, 'I'm not going to say anything to this person, they are going to think I'm crazy.' But when we do, the Holy Spirit comes and does something amazing with that person. We just speak boldly, you know, with love. We're not there to beat people over the head, we're there to share the love of God and see people come to Christ.

My goodness, we were just thinking about this the other night – digressing slightly here – but there's a film called *Zoolander*, I think there's a second one coming out. Some people may never have heard of this film – it's a bit crazy – but there's a person in that by the name of David Bowie. I'm sure you've all heard of David Bowie, and that film was shot 15 years ago and you think, 'He looks great in this movie, 15 years ago,' but he just died this year. Now 15 years: you think, is it that long since that film's been made? Now it doesn't seem that long (although it was) but we're all getting older, every single one of us and nobody knows how long we're going to be on this earth. We don't know do we, and we've had many times when we've been in a place and shared the gospel with someone and we don't know if today is this person's last day on earth or if they will live to a ripe old age. We don't know. So we just pray that God guides our steps today. We're not here to beat people, to make them become Christians. This is *good news,* isn't it? Good news, the gospel. There's plenty of rubbish out there on the television. If people are watching EastEnders, they are going to get an East End life, aren't they? Rubbish in, rubbish out. So we want to give people good news.

[Terry] Isn't that good testimony, eh? It was amazing! And do you know the thing was, we'd eaten in IHOP and then we were going back to the car, and then I saw the lady having a smoke and I said, 'I've just got to go. I've got to go back.' And I went back to her and that's when I say, 'Has anybody told you that God loves you and Jesus died for you; that he's got a plan for your life?' So that's the tack we're going to be using today. We're going to be using the script and 'Has anybody ever told you God loves you, Jesus died for you and has a plan for your life?' That's how we start. Whether the answer is 'No' or 'Yes', ask, 'Can I just talk you through this?' That's how we do it. 'Has anybody told you God loves you? The Bible says we've all sinned, Jesus has died for you, and would you like to decide whether or not you want to live for God?' It's that simple; really that simple. Keep taking them back to the script if they try and take you away, about church or this or that. Take them back to the script. Would you mind if I pray with you and for you? Most people will say, 'OK, pray for me,' so you pray. *Dear Lord, just bless [Kevin / Harry / Louise], bless them, bless their family, give them a long life, and satisfy them.'* I just pray some scriptural stuff and then *'I pray they will receive you quickly. Amen.'*

Well if they say that – because, it's interesting, it's a good question, and it's a good point because people do say that – 'Will you pray for me?' – I always say yes and just start praying for them. If they ask you to pray for them, pray for them. This is where we need to be on the front foot, right? Of course, we go in love, but be on the front foot. I mean people say that to me, 'Will you please pray for me?' so I say, 'Yes, let's just bow your head right now.' Do you know what I mean? Because otherwise it's just religious, it's rubbish.

If they are going somewhere, ask if you can walk with them and pray with them. Do that, OK? That's what we do. I've known people get led to Christ while just walking down the street with them to the Tube or whatever. Seriously. So it's like eliminating 'excusia' and using 'exousia' – which is 'delegated empowerment' or 'authority and conferred influential power' and we're going step out in that power. Acts 1:8 says, 'But you will receive power when the Holy Spirit comes on you; and you will be my witnesses' . . . in Thamesmead, in Woolwich, in south London, wherever! The uttermost parts of the earth. We're actually at the uttermost part of the earth today!

You can use the same principle with your family, of course! It's a good principle. I've led my mum to the Lord, I've led two sisters to the Lord. I'm still going for my two brothers! But, this is a great tool because it depersonalises it from you, because they know you, they know how to navigate and wrestle you, like wrestling a bear. And it might be like that today for some of you, if you are thinking, 'Oh well I've tried that, done that,' whatever, fighting fear and all that, but you'll get an anointing from God and you can go and do it. And this is a proven tool, you know what I mean? So just keep taking them back to the script. We're going to practise on one another in a short while.

Of course, if you have some cards for the local church you can give them out, and anybody who does accept Christ and you pray with them, give them a card to the church, or invite them to church if you like. If you are visiting an area and don't know of a specific local church, the best guidance to give people who are looking to find a church is to tell them to look for one that is Christ-centred and Bible-based.

But while the church is immensely important, try for this moment in time, to forget church. Seriously, in this moment, we're winning souls, and let me tell you something before we start practising on each other. I was on the back streets of Manchester, I was addicted to drugs, was a drug dealer, a criminal. People would keep away from me; I was quite dangerous. I thought I ran the estate, like one of the estates round here, and we'd sit in front of the shops, me and my guys, friends, thinking we run things. And this guy used to come and say, 'God loves you, Jesus died for you and he's got a plan for your life.' He'd look me in the eye with boldness and courage. He came to me and told me that. Everybody else tried to take the mickey out of him and I said, 'No, listen. I want to listen to this guy.' So somebody came and told me about Jesus. He didn't mention church, no church at all. Shortly afterwards, I went to his house. He led me to Christ:

'God loves you, Jesus died for you and has a plan for your life. Do you want to turn from your sin? Do you want to receive Christ as your Saviour?'

'Yes I do.' I got down on my knees and prayed the prayer, right then and there.

Of course, he followed me up, but I didn't particularly feel like I needed to be followed up. The Holy Spirit followed me up, do you know what I'm saying? What does the Bible say? It doesn't say go and 'just' invite them to church. Amen. Is that right? You see this is simple: it says go and preach the gospel. That's all it says to do, do you know what I mean?

So today we're fulfilling the great commission. We're going to go and share the good news and we're going to lead people to Christ. Amen. So all I'm doing is cutting through, like, preconditioning and training for most people who haven't led zip to Christ – do you know what I mean? Haven't led anybody to Christ. They just haven't done it and they are full of excusia, and they are full of religion and they are full of dead men's bones. But I tell you something: when you go and share the good news, I can feel the anointing right now, because when you share the good news, it does you more good than them! Think about it! 'Wow, God loves me, Jesus died for me, he's got a plan for my life, wow.' You know what I mean? Come on, it's great isn't it? So you're reaffirming the gospel in your own life and Acts 1:8 – 'and you shall be witnesses when this power comes upon you'. When you witness to the power of God, the power comes. I'm like this all the time. The gospel is the power of God unto salvation. First to them who believe. Amen. So if it's first to them who believe, that's you who believe, that's me. That's the scripture, isn't it?

The gospel is the power of God unto salvation. Wholeness, fullness, *sozo*, peace, *shalom*, nothing missing, nothing broken. First to them who believe. Everything I need, and everything you need, is in the gospel. Isn't that amazing? It's not out there, it's not in this, that, whatever. It's in the gospel and that can be in me, totally whole. Are you encouraged? Right, what we'll do now is split into twos and practise on each other. You can be resistant but not too much, OK? Jill and I will demonstrate first, and then the rest of you can split into pairs and then we'll practise and train.

[Terry] Hello, what's your name?

[Jill] Jill.

[Terry] Nice to meet you, I'm Terry. Good to see you. We're just doing some talking, if you've got a couple of minutes. Has anybody told you that God loves you? They have? Well that's great, that's good. Well, I'm here to encourage you today and tell you that God loves you, Jesus died for you and he's got a plan for your life. Do you mind if I just talk you through this? It's just four points. OK. The Bible says that God loves you; that we have all sinned – we've fallen short of the glory of God – but Jesus came and died for us so that we can be restored to God and have total forgiveness. Yes, that's right. The fourth point is that we need to decide to live for God and there's a prayer here we can pray. Would you mind if I just prayed a quick prayer with you? OK. I'll pray a quick prayer. 'Lord, I thank you for Jill, I pray you'll bless her, bless her family, give her long life, protect her and do good in her life. And I pray she'll come to know you and accept you quickly. Amen.' Would you like to accept Christ today? Would you like me to pray with you and for you? Would you like to receive forgiveness? Well, I've just explained it to you. God loves you . . .

[Jill] But I'm a good person.

[Terry] Well, this is what a lot of people say, but the Bible says we've all sinned and fallen short of the glory of God. The wages of sin is death but the gift of God is eternal life. So that's why we need forgiveness from sin. Jesus died for us. I can pray with you and for you right now and we'll pray and you can accept Christ. Good, yes, Amen. Just pray this prayer after me. 'Dear Lord Jesus, please forgive me, come into my life, help me live for you, fill me with your Holy Spirit, in the name of Jesus. Amen.' Wonderful, that's great. Well I'd like to give you this; you can take that with you and we can also invite you to our local church. We have a meeting tonight.

Give Jill a round of applause, she's just got saved again. OK, Jill's going to demonstrate on me now.

[Jill] What I'd probably say is to just check with someone that it's OK to touch them. Terry knew it was OK to take my hand but when you don't know the person, just always ask first. You can be bold and say, 'Is it OK to touch your arm?' If you don't feel like you want to, then just do what you feel comfortable with and whatever the other person feels comfortable with.

[Jill] Hello there.

[Terry] Hey up.

[Jill] You don't sound like you're from London? You're from up North. We like people from up North. Can I ask you a question? Did you know that God loves you, Jesus died for you and has got a plan for your life? Has anyone ever told you that? That's good. Would you like to know more? Well, the Bible says that we've all sinned and all fallen short of God's measure, that we've missed the mark. Well, let me just show you this. I'm going to give you this as a free gift. Says here a big heart, because God loves me, but it also says a big X – I have sinned, which means we've fallen short of the glory of God, but Jesus has made a way because he died for us! But now we've got to decide to live for God. Do you mind if I pray for you? Is it OK that I just put my hand on your arm? 'Lord, we thank you for Terry, for his life. We thank you that you want to bless him and his family and bless everything he does in the name of Jesus. We thank you for it. Come and touch him today, Lord, and I hope he accepts you quickly.' Would you like the gift of salvation? Then we're going to say this pray, the prayer on the script.